Capacity Management in MRP, APS & S&OP Software

Shaun Snapp

For information about this title or to order other books and/or electronic media, contact the publisher:

SCM Focus Press
PO Box 29502 #9059
Las Vegas, NV 89126-9502
http://www.scmfocus.com/scmfocuspress
(408) 657-0249

ISBN: 978-1-939731-14-2

Printed in the United States of America

Contents

CHAPTER 1

Introduction

In this book, we'll repeatedly touch upon two subjects:

1. *Short-Term Capacity Management:* Capacity leveling or capacity constraining, which is the movement of demand to fit within the available supply; and

2. *Long-Term Capacity Management:* Capacity planning is the

comparison of long term supply versus long-term demand in order to determine if the capacity should be changed.

That's why we've called this book *Capacity Management*, as it covers both capacity leveling/capacity constraining and capacity planning.

It's a near universal practice to present these two processes in separate contexts, but they are, in fact, closely related such that understanding either one helps in understanding the other. For example, while software models both Short-Term Capacity Management and Long-Term Capacity Management, it can automatically perform the former while merely supporting the manual determination of the latter. Additionally, while the former is about **respecting system limitations**, the latter is about **evaluating system limitations** to determine if they should be changed. Obviously, you can't both simultaneously respect system limitations and question them.

In the modern era, we support both processes by entering constraints into a computer system and loading either real or predicted demand upon the constraints. This is a simplification, though, because in reality, many complexities interfere with both processes, the most common of which relate to the accuracy of demand and capacity information. A common example would be forecasted demand which, except in built-to-order manufacturing environments, is naturally probabilistic.

And so capacity information is nearly always inaccurate to some degree because:

1. Capacity information can change after resources are first setup.
2. Capacity information can fall out-of-date with what exists in reality.
3. Resources that exist and are modeled can go out for unplanned maintenance or provide less capacity than was originally modeled.
4. Many types of capacity are **not normally modeled in software** (though the application such ability) due to the effort required to do so.
5. Some type of capacities simply can't be modeled or modeled properly in software.

Capacity leveling and constraining are simply **two different approaches** of moving loads from excess demand to surplus supply. This can be simple, such as moving demand on the same set of resources along a planning horizon, or it can be more sophisticated, such as moving capacity amongst alternate resources. As the SCM Focus Press book *Superplant: Creating a Nimble Manufacturing Enterprise with Adaptive Planning Software* addresses, the most advanced approach involves moving demand excess amongst alternate resources in different manufacturing plants.

Capacity leveling, the older of the two approaches, can be performed without computers. Capacity constraining, the more sophisticated approach, requires computers as it must follow rules configured in the software.

According to Wikipedia, capacity planning involves two main considerations:

1. Capacity planning is a long-term decision that establishes a firm's overall level of resources. It extends over the time horizon long enough to obtain resources.

2. Inadequate capacity planning can lead to the loss of customers and business. Excess capacity can drain company resources and prevent investments into more lucrative ventures.

Let's examine each consideration in detail.

1. *Long-Term in Nature:* Capacity planning is long term in nature because it involves not simply moving demand, but also **adjusting system capacity.** Usually in nearer-term planning, fewer changes can be made to actual capacity. In contrast, long-term planning utilizes strategies of capacity leveling and constraining.

    a. *Lead Time and Prediction Issues:* Take a factory, for example, where if in the near term demand exceeds supply, it's unreasonable to buy new machines, install them, and take all the other necessary steps to support the high demand. Indeed, it's unreasonable not only because of the long lead-time to take these steps, but also because it can't be determined within the near term whether such investments are worthwhile. The option, therefore, in the near (and mid) term usually involves either "moving" the demand by postponing production from the time it would ordinarily be scheduled if capacity were unlimited, or moving it to an alternative capacity, or doing both. However, capacity planning means questioning constraints -- possibly *adding* capacity – and, therefore, this tends to be a question for the long term.

b. *Flexible Capacity:* When capacity can be added very easily and quickly, the need for capacity planning is unnecessary. These situations, though, are uncommon, and there are more limitations to be found as demand increases versus capacity.

2. The Balance: Capacity planning, at its core, is the balance of over-investment and under-investment.

a. If capacity does not increase and demand exceeds forecast, then opportunities will be lost – under-investment.

b. If capacity does increase and demand falls short of forecast, then investments will be lost – over-investment.

Different software and different planning processes support these two different capacity processes.

Supply chain planning, on the other hand, accomplishes **capacity leveling or constraining.** Systems that do this are called MRP (Material Requirements Planning) and APS (Advanced Planning and Scheduling) systems. Their activities occur within the supply-planning and production-planning modules.

1. MRP systems can only perform capacity leveling.

2. APS can perform either capacity leveling or capacity constraining.

Types of planning performed in supply and initial production can aptly be called "planning threads" as they're sometimes referred to as "planning runs". In fact, there may be multiple planning runs within any planning thread. Therefore, the term "planning thread" is far more accurate than the term "planning run."

There are five major planning threads that make up supply planning (and initial production planning process):

1. *S&OP and Rough-Cut Capacity Plan:* These planning runs are used for long-range planning and, in most cases, are offline analyses and are not part of the live environment.

2. *The Network/Initial Supply Plan* (performed by MRP in ERP systems):This produces the initial production and procurement plan. It's focused on bringing stock into the supply network and in creating stock with planned production orders. It can also be called the master production schedule (MPS) if the initial supply plan is run under certain criteria. (We cover this later.)

3. *Capacity Leveling Plan:* If an unconstrained method is used to create the network/initial supply plan, then a second planning run may be performed to spread out the demand so that it matches with capacity. If, on the other hand, a capacity constraining method is used, then this second step or planning run is not performed. Therefore, the existence of this planning run depends on the method used for the network/initial-planning run.

4. *The Deployment Plan* (performed by DRP in ERP systems or in APS systems with a heuristic or with optimization):Deployment is focused on pushing stock from locations at the beginning of the supply network to the end of the supply network. While a number of applications can perform either capacity leveling or capacity constraining for the deployment run, in practice, using anything but lot sizing and target stock levels is extremely uncommon. (We will not cover this later.)

5. *The Redeployment Plan* (performed by specialized applications with redeployment functionality or with a custom report):This plan focuses on repositioning stock already in the supply network to locations where it has a higher probability of consumption. As with the deployment plan, the redeployment plan addresses the application of capacity leveling or capacity constraining.

The frequencies of the different supply planning and initial production planning threads vary:

Planning Thread	Timing
Rough Cut Capacity Plan / S&OP Run	Weekly to Monthly
Network/Initial Supply Plan	Daily to Weekly
Capacity Leveling Plan	Daily to Weekly
Deployment Plan	Daily to Weekly
Redeployment Plan	Weekly to Quarterly

Capacity planning is far less structured in both its process and in the software that it uses than capacity leveling and constraining. S&OP is the most common process involving capacity planning, although it also branches into other areas that are beyond simply capacity planning, such as capacity budgeting. S&OP is the most collaborative of the planning processes and is designed to be the process by which sales, operations, and finance collaborate to determine the planning activities. This is necessary because when budget changes become necessary, finance must be included. Sales and operations already collaborate – at least somewhat as sales forecasts are often melded into the supply chain forecast to generate the supply chain forecast.

S&OP has several attributes:

- *Connecting the Business:* S&OP is all about connectivity – connecting together different corporate branches, as well as connecting plans at the **top** and **bottom** of an organization or at the most detailed level.

- *High-Level Planning:* S&OP is the second highest level of company planning, strategic planning being the highest.

- *Balancing Act:* S&OP is intended to help companies determine how to both balance the orientations of sales, operations, and finance, and to do things like adding capacity to meet projected demand.

- *Capacity Treatment and Financial Focus:* In a real S&OP environment, the constraints are evaluated. For instance, if demand is predicted to increase, then finance may not only rely upon internal funds, but may "go to the bank" to borrow money to fund capacity changes. The question is, does the captured excess demand have the profitability to justify capacity change? S&OP also has one of the longest average planning horizons of any of the planning processes, second only to strategic planning.

- *Aggregation:* S&OP should be an aggregated form of planning, although it does need to feed down to actual impact on individual "modeled" resources, as well as extrapolated to un-modeled resources.

S&OP impacts long-term decisions on the planning horizon:

> *"The immediate, short, medium, long and very long time frame forecasts should be tied to specific resource decisions. The immediate time frame forecast should be the basis for material changes and the schedule changes. These decisions are reactions to specific changes in demand forecast. The short decision time frame is used to make specific changes in the number of workers. The medium decision time frame is used for making equipment changes (purchase or disposal). The decision to bring in new equipment is based on meeting competitive objectives. The long term decision time frame is used for substantial changes in technology."*
> – Sales Forecasting for Strategic Resource Planning

The Use of Screen Shots in the Book

I consult in some popular and well-known applications, and I've found that companies have often been given the wrong impression of an application's capabilities. As part of my consulting work, I am required to present the results of testing various applications. The research may show that a well-known application is not able to perform some functionality well enough to be used by a company, and point to a lesser-known application where this functionality is easily performed. Because I am routinely in this situation, I am asked to provide evidence of the testing results within applications, and screen shots provide this necessary evidence.

Furthermore, some time ago, it became a habit for me to include extensive screen shots in most of my project documentation. A screen shot does not, of course, guarantee that a particular functionality works, but it is the best that can be done in a document format. Everything in this book exists in one application or another, and nothing described in this book is hypothetical.

How Writing Bias Is Controlled at SCM Focus and SCM Focus Press

Bias is a serious problem in the enterprise software field. Large vendors receive uncritical coverage of their products, and large consulting companies recommend the large vendors that have the resources to hire and pay consultants rather than the vendors with the best software for the client's needs.

At SCM Focus, we have yet to financially benefit from a company's decision to buy an application showcased in print, either in a book or on the SCM Focus website. This may change in the future as SCM Focus grows – but we have been writing with a strong viewpoint for years without coming into any conflicts of interest. SCM Focus has the most stringent rules related to controlling bias and restricting commercial influence of any information provider. These "writing rules" are provided in the link below:

http://www.scmfocus.com/writing-rules/

The Approach to the Book

By writing this book, I wanted to help people get exactly the information they need without having to read a lengthy volume. The approach to the book is essentially the same as to my previous books, and in writing this book I followed the same principles.

1. **Be direct and concise.** There is very little theory in this book and the math that I cover is simple. While the mathematics behind the optimization methods for supply and production planning is involved, there are plenty of books, which cover this topic. This book is focused on software and for most users and implementers of the software the most important thing to understand is conceptually what the software is doing.

2. **Based on project experience.** Nothing in the book is hypothetical; I have worked with it or tested it on an actual project. My project experience has led to my understanding a number of things that are not covered in typical supply planning books. In this book, I pass on this understanding to you.

3. **Saturate the book with graphics.** Roughly two-thirds of a human's

sensory input is visual,and books that do not use graphics—especially educational and training books such as this one—can fall short of their purpose. Graphics have also been used consistently and extensively on the SCM Focus website.

Important Terminology
This book will use a variety of terminology that it is necessary to know in order to understand the book. These terms are divided into different categories.

The SCM Focus Site
As I am also the author of the SCM Focus site, http://www.scmfocus.com, the site and the book share a number of concepts and graphics. Furthermore, this book contains many links to articles on the site, which provide more detail on specific subjects. This book provides an explanation of how supply and production planning software works and aims to continue to be a reference after its initial reading. However,if your interest in supply planning software continues to grow, the SCM Focus site is a good resource to which articles are continually added.

http://www.scmfocus.com/

Intended Audience
This book is for anyone interested in better understanding safety stock and service level and, particularly, how to improve how they are set. However, the book also should be of interest to anyone that works in supply chain management systems – both ERP and external planning systems. A final group that could benefit from the book would be those that manage supply chain departments.

If you have any questions or comments on the book, please e-mail me at shaunsnapp@scmfocus.com.

Abbreviations
A listing of all abbreviations used throughout the book is provided at the end of the book.

CHAPTER 2

Capacity Leveling

Introduction

Materials Requirements Planning, or MRP, was the first supply planning method to be computerized. MRP can create purchase requisitions and initial production requisitions. However, MRP does not have the information necessary to schedule production and is not aware of production constraints. For this reason, I like to call MRP a method for "initial" planning only and production requisitions created by MRP should be considered a first pass only. These production requisitions are really just translations of demand quantities and dates adjusted for lead times. Either they must be capacity-leveled in the ERP system, or sent to a production planning and scheduling system.

Of the hardware constraints mentioned previously been lifted, although more and more options become available with every passing year. Reorder point methods are still used to control procurement and sometimes production; however, they now work with MRP to create economic order quantities. Even though MRP is mathematically simple, it performs a number of repetitive calculations that, prior to MRP, had to be calculated manually—a very tedious task. Converting large volumes of sales orders into production orders and purchase orders was quite a feat when this capability was first developed independently in the early 1960s at J. I. CASE and Stanley Tools. Yet, quite a few companies continued using their old systems before industry converted over to MRP in the late 1970s.

What MRP Includes

The easiest way to understand MRP is to understand what is included in the MRP calculation that generates production and procurement orders:

- Sales Orders

- Purchase Orders

- Materials

- Stock (There are many different types of stock, but only unrestricted and valuated stock can be included in MRP. In addition, while optional, MRP should be set to incorporate the stock in transit.)

- Material Lead Times

- Components

- Assemblies

- Lot Size

- Resources/Work Centers

What MRP Does Not Include

MRP is very simple; it has fewer options and configuration requirements when compared to the other methods for performing initial planning (production and procurement planning). Therefore, it is also useful to understand what MRP does not include.

- *Normal Stock Transfers*: Notice that unlike APS or DRP, MRP does not create stock transfers. This is because it has no concept of the relationships between facilities and is not a method for deployment.

- *Inventory Balancing Stock Transfers*: MRP does not rebalance inventory to meet future demand the way several supply planning methods do.

- *Prioritization:* MRP does not understand priority; it only understands quantities, dates and lead times. Consequently, if a high-priority customer places an order for product later than a low-priority customer, the low-priority customer receives the inventory. However, many companies operate based on customer priority in addition to the need date, so this is where inventory is either manually allocated or allocation software comes into the equation.

- *Constraints:* One of the great limitations of MRP—and one of the main reasons that constraint-based planning was developed and flourished in the late 1990s—is that it does not know what is feasible; rather it works backward from requirements and simply develops a plan based upon this figure.

A screenshot of the MRP setup in SAP ERP demonstrates MRP's simplicity and how few options require configuration.

Single-Item, Single-Level

Material	SCM Focus Mat
MRP Area	3800
Plant	AC00

MRP control parameters

Processing key	NETCH	Net change for total horizon
Create purchase req.	2	Purchase requisitions in opening period
Delivery schedules	3	Schedule lines
Create MRP list	1	MRP list
Planning mode	1	Adapt planning data (normal mode)
Scheduling	1	Basic dates will be determined for plann
Planning date	27.03.2012	

Process control parameters
☐ Display results before they are saved

- The first option is the processing key, which relates to whether MRP will reprocess everything (called regenerative planning) or whether it will just perform a net change.

- The second option relates to whether purchase requisitions are within the planning horizon. If purchase requisitions are not created by the system, they can be created manually. One option here allows only planned orders to be created outside the planning horizon.

- The delivery schedule setting controls if and how schedule lines will be created.

- The next setting relates to whether or not an MRP List should be created.

- The MRP List is the list of the MRP output per material.

- The planning-mode setting controls whether the system re-explodes the BOM after each run. This is performed when the BOM for the assembly has changed, and/or the quantity or date of the procurement proposal has changed.

- The scheduling setting controls how dates are determined for planned orders and whether only a basic method will be used to determine the dates of planned orders or whether a more complex method involving lead time scheduling and capacity planning will be used.

As you can see, the options are limited and several are related to such things as reprocessing all orders, determining when to create procurement orders, etc. By contrast, the SNP Network Heuristic has many more controls, including something called "Low Level Codes," which controls the sequence in which the product-location combinations are run. This is described in detail below:

http://www.scmfocus.com/sapplanning/2011/02/04/level-of-bom-planning-in-the-snp-heuristic-and-low-level-codes/

Many companies rely upon SAP ERP to run their MRP, and SAP has a good description of the mechanics of MRP:

> *The system calculates net requirements for all the requirement quantities that are to be planned. The system thereby compares*

available warehouse stock or the scheduled receipts from purchasing and production with planned independent requirements, material reservations and incoming sales orders. In the case of a material shortage, that is, if the available stock (including firmed receipts) is smaller than the quantity required, the system creates procurement proposals.

— SAP MRP Uses and Their Implications

Major Functionality of MRP

Understanding MRP is a great place to start for understanding the other supply planning methods. The major functionality in MRP is shown in the graphic below.

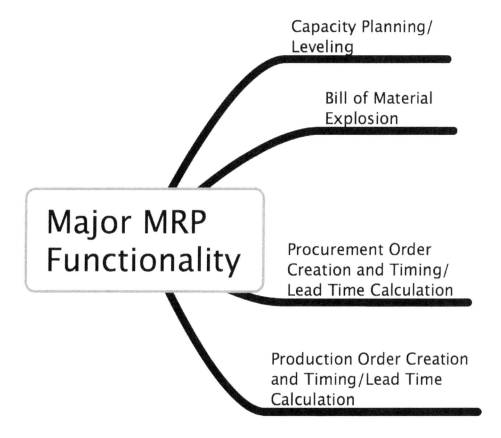

MRP covers the functions listed above. MRP's functionality is basic arithmetic; however, it does so for many products at once, and can be re-run quickly compared to other supply planning methods.

Manufacturing Capacity Leveling/Planning

Capacity leveling/planning is the activity of spreading or moving production orders from periods where there is no capacity to periods where there is capacity.[1] Capacity leveling can be carried out with all of the supply planning methods described in this book. Even when capacities are constrained (such as with cost optimization and allocation), it is often still necessary to perform manual capacity leveling as the resource master data is never one hundred percent accurate.

When infinite capacity planning is configured, capacity leveling is frequently performed with a capacity leveling heuristic. Capacity leveling heuristics have the following limitations:

- They do not take into account dependent demands in the leveling process. Leveling is only performed locally on a resource, sometimes leading to overloaded resources, and on-hand stocks or shortfall quantities. Because of its more limited nature, the overall result of capacity leveling is less comprehensive than constraint-based planning.

- Infinite capacity planning with capacity leveling is less automated than a system that is capacity constrained. A capacity-constrained system, because it is automated, allows for more planning re-runs without the necessity of rechecking the capacity consumption.

Keeping in mind the above limitations, it is also important to remember few companies are using constraint-based planning (which is the opposite approach from capacity leveling) or—if they have implemented a constraint-based planning approach—few are using it successfully. .

A description of capacity leveling and SAP is available at this link.
   http://www.scmfocus.com/sapplanning/2008/05/08/capacity-leveling-in-snp/

---

[1] When capacity leveling is added to MRP, this can be referred to as MRP II. A number of books draw a distinction between MRP and MRP II; however I don't see the term MRP II used in industry, and MRP II involves several other components such as reporting. I don't find MRP II to be a useful concept, so I don't cover it in this book.

Backward and Forward Scheduling

Change View "SNP Capacity Leveling: Parameter Profile": Overview

New Entries

SNP Capacity Leveling: Parameter Profile					
Capacity Leveling Profile	Cap.Method	Scheduing Direction	Level Fxd	Set Fixing	
SCM FOCUS PROFILE	Heuristic Method	Combined Forward a	☑	☑	▲
					▼

The same view continues by scrolling to the right in the application.

Change View "SNP Capacity Leveling: Parameter Profile": Overview

New Entries

SNP Capacity Leveling: Parameter Profile			
Capacity Leveling Profile	Priority	Sort Seq.	
SCM FOCUS PROFILE	Order Size	Ascending	▲
			▼

In SAP APO SNP, there is an area to set up profiles, which can be used to perform capacity leveling. Options in the profiles include whether the leveling will be forward only or both forward and backward, whether priorities should be used, and what the sort sequence should be, in addition to other controls. More details are available in the article below.

http://www.scmfocus.com/sapplanning/2008/05/08/capacity-leveling-in-snp/

Capacity leveling can also be performed in the PP (Production Planning) module of SAP ERP, although its functionality is more limited.

http://www.scmfocus.com/sapplanning/2008/05/08/capacity-planning-and-constraint-based-planning-for-service-parts/

The Importance of the Planning Time Horizon
In addition to running the critical items prior to the less-critical items, the planning time horizon determines how far forward in the MPS run the critical items are able to consume capacity. This is an important, but sometimes overlooked feature of the planning time horizon. By pushing the MPS planning time horizon

out further than the MRP runs, greater priority is given to the MPS items, which is what most companies tend to desire.

Conclusion

MRP was the first computerized supply planning method to be developed. MRP is simple, but was an important first step at reducing much of the busy work involved with supply planning. DRP and, to a lesser degree, supply planning heuristics are related to MRP. While MRP is concerned with the inbound movement of material into a location for the purposes of production, DRP is concerned with the flows of material between locations and supply planning heuristics can be used both for the initial plan and for deployment. MRP is not capacity constrained and creates an infinite and thus infeasible plan. This means that the results of MRP cannot ordinarily all be met by the company or by the company's suppliers. To make MRP results realistic, both material and resource limitations are introduced with capacity leveling. This, however, is only one of MRP's limitations; there are several limitations related to MRP and DRP that are primarily related to their simplified assumptions. These limitations motivated the development of APS software for supply planning.

CHAPTER 3

Constraint-based Planning

Background

Constraint-based planning (or finite planning) puts limiters on the capacity that can be allocated to various resources. Using constraints means setting up inequalities in the system that reduces the solution space to what is feasible. An important distinction between the APS supply planning method of heuristics and the methods of allocation and cost optimization is that the latter two can be performed in a constrained way. Constraint-based planning works by setting up resources, which can be anything from factory equipment to transportation units to handling equipment, in the model. Resources are then assigned limitations in capacity and/or availability (e.g., they have a specific capacity and can only be run from 8 a.m. to 10 p.m.). The goal is to match the resources as closely as possible to the realities of the environment being modeled. Unlike unconstrained or infinite planning—which will allocate requirements to a resource per the requests from the order management system, determined strictly by order dates—constraint-based planning moves orders when resources become filled, which means (assuming the resources represent reality) a plan generated in this way is feasible and implementable.

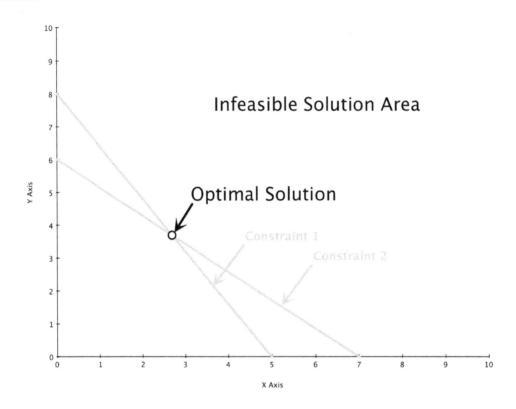

When used in planning, constraints limit the solution to what is feasible, or what is action-able by the business. By limiting the solution, the time and processing spent evaluating recommendations that cannot be converted in reality are also limited.

Different domains of the supply chain have different types of resources that must be modeled. For instance, trucks are a resource for supply planning, while a workstation is a resource for production planning. However, all resources work similarly in that they have a capacity, which can be declared to the planning system. With unconstrained planning (or infinite planning), capacities may or may not be declared—and, if they are declared, there is nothing to stop the system from placing an unlimited load on any resource. With constraint-based planning, three things happen: (1) resources are both declared, (2) at least one of the resources in each process chain has its capacity constrained or capped, and (3) the system can only load the resource up to that cap before moving further loads to a different time or to an alternative resource. Of the different supply planning methods, only allocation and cost optimization have the *ability to run in a constrained* fashion.

However, this occurs only if the system is configured to manage resources in a finite manner. It is important to understand the distinction between what any system is capable of doing and what it is actually doing in a specific implementation. (This mistake is made in many areas of software evaluation, for instance, it is often stated that an application has a capability of doing something, but this does not say anything about how effective the functionality is, or how difficult or easy it is to configure or to maintain.)

Many years ago, it took me four separate meetings with a group of users to convert a portion of them (and I was never able to convince them all) to the understanding that the production planning system they thought was performing constraint-based planning was actually unconstrained, as none of the resources in the system were configured to activate this functionality. It is quite typical for many of the resources that are assigned to a product to be unconstrained in a production planning and scheduling system. Frequently, only the most restricted resource or "bottleneck resource" is constrained. The bottleneck resource is the pacesetter for the overall processing of the product. However, if no resources for a product are constrained, then the planning for that product—at least at that location—is infinite. The graphic on the next page describes how bottleneck resources work:

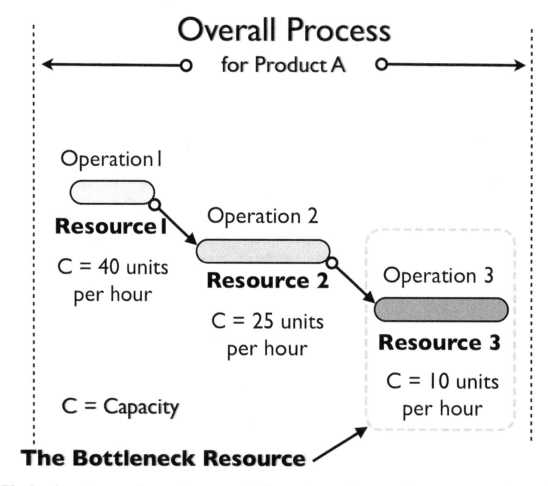

Overall Process
for Product A

Operation 1

Resource 1

C = 40 units
per hour

Operation 2

Resource 2

C = 25 units
per hour

Operation 3

Resource 3

C = 10 units
per hour

C = Capacity

The Bottleneck Resource

The bottleneck operation and resource is Operation 3. Because Resource 3 produces the lowest amount of units per hour, it restricts the capacity of the overall process, or sequence, to ten units per hour. The overall process cannot exceed the capacity of the slowest resource (unless the slowest resource runs for more hours per day than the rest of the resources). For this reason, it is unnecessary to constrain the capacity of either Resource 1 or Resource 2. This is the standard example and typically applies to a manufacturing problem.

The Types of Constraints Commonly Used by Supply Planning Systems

The concept of constraining resources transfers as well to supply planning as it does to production planning. Constraint-based planning actually began in production planning and scheduling, and migrated into supply planning. However, supply planning and production planning are significantly different. Production planning models a sequence of activities that are implemented by resources. In discrete manufacturing, the activities are most often directly sequential (one resource completes a process and the next resource begins work on the material). In true process manufacturing (as opposed to mixing operations), the resources are still sequential, but they are lagged and the overall sequence is more complex than in discrete manufacturing. In these scenarios, production planning can be easily throttled or constrained by the resource with the lowest capacity along the line, the so-called bottleneck resource. The sequential and interdependent nature of the production line allows it to be effectively constrained by one resource, meaning that it is only necessary to model one resource along the entire line.

How Supply Planning Resources Differ from Production Planning Resources
Unlike production resources, supply planning resources (storage, location, shipping and receiving, and transportation) are not in a sequential line. When each is used, supply planning resources have substantial lags between them, and they are also much more flexible in that they are less prone to absolute constraints. Clearly, the production planning constraining requirement is a much easier one to meet than the requirement of constraining supply planning resources. Therefore, the most common resources to be constrained in supply planning systems are not supply planning resources, but production resources, although they are of less detail than the same production resources that are entered into the production planning system.

To read more about finite and bottleneck resources see this post below:

http://www.scmfocus.com/sapplanning/2009/07/01/bottleneck-resources/

To read more about the types of resources that are included in supply planning systems see this post below:

http://www.scmfocus.com/supplyplanning/2011/10/02/commonly-used-and-unused-constraints-for-supply-planning/

Important Considerations for Constraint-based Systems
Let me continue the story of my attempt to convince planners of the unconstrained nature of their implementation. I showed them screenshots of the configuration, which clearly showed that constraining was not taking place. However, I still faced significant doubters in the audience, primarily because they had been told by the company's executives—incorrectly as it turns out—that the application they were using performed constraint-based planning. The doubters said that what I was saying could not be correct because the system in question was simply "designed to perform constraint-based planning." This statement was true—the system was designed to perform constraint-based planning. However, the system still needed to be set up properly to constrain the plan by resources, and the system they had just implemented had not been set up to do this. For some time, this company struggled with trying to figure out why the only limiting factor in production was the lot size at the product-location combination. This project turned out to be the first of several projects that I worked on where at least a few people in the business thought that the system was constraining the plan based upon resources when it was not, in some cases years after the system had initially gone live.

Because of experiences such as the one I describe above, I want to state clearly that any system that can perform constrained planning can also perform unconstrained planning. It simply depends on whether the configuration for constraint-based planning is selected. Even experienced professionals trip up on this fact when describing constraint-based planning.

Hypothetically, heuristics could be used to perform constraint-based planning, although I am unaware of a system that works in this way. Heuristics work with a two-step process: one heuristic or a set of heuristics is used to assign loads to resources, and then a second, specialized, capacity-leveling heuristic is used to level the loads (or manual capacity leveling is performed). Allocation and cost optimization *can* both be performed with constraint resources, but they do not need to be. Also, do not assume that every company that has implemented allocation or cost optimization is actually performing constraint-based planning.

Some specific examples of supply planning constraints include the following:

- The maximum amount of material that can be placed in a truck

- The maximum number of miles a truck can drive in a day
- The maximum output available from a piece of machinery
- The maximum amount a bin at a warehouse can hold
- The maximum amount of material a warehouse in total can hold
- The time windows (i.e., calendar) that is acceptable for material delivery for production facilities, warehouses, and retail locations

These constraints above represent the declared capacity in the system. When the resources are set to finite, the optimizer or the allocation system can load, but not exceed, the declared capacity. With constrained resources, once capacity is reached in one period, the optimizer attempts to move the load backward or forward in time, meaning the product will be available earlier or later than the requirements date. Without accurate constraint data, the plan output will be incorrect and demands will be allocated to periods where there is, in fact, no capacity or moved from areas where capacity is available.

Maintaining the data about resources and the parameters, or master data maintenance, is often thought of as independent of the planning system—that is, the master data on resource constraint information must be maintained by humans. However, master data maintenance can be considered quite system dependent as some systems make master data more difficult to maintain than do others. I have come to the conclusion that there is no reason all planning systems should not be able to upload spreadsheets especially when used in prototype mode, which allows planners to constantly update resource information in a format that makes sense to them. I have more on this topic at the link below:

http://www.scmfocus.com/supplychainmasterdata/2011/05/methodology-for-adjusting-master-data/

In this chapter, we have spent a good amount of time covering whether or not a system is capacity-constrained. What must also be addressed is the accuracy of the resource information that is entered into the planning system. Inaccurate resource information undermines the overall constraint-based planning process because individual planners must go into the system and perform manual capacity leveling in areas where there is inaccuracy. At a certain level of inaccuracy, it simply makes more sense to turn off constraint-based planning. Unfortunately, many more companies have the desire to perform constraint-based planning than have the willingness to fund the maintenance of constraint master data.

Production Batch Sizes Versus Full Resource Constraints

Supply planning maintains an overlap with production planning in that the batch sizes (i.e., lot sizes) set for production planning serve to batch orders for the supply plan when using any of the supply planning methods. Furthermore, resource constraints, which are more detailed than lot sizes, can also be included when using either the allocation or cost optimization methods. There are two main reasons as to why production constraints should be included with resource constraints in a supply planning system rather than relying upon production lot sizes:

1. **To constrain the plan to a feasible schedule.** Production lot sizes simply declare the batch in which an order must be produced (500 units, 1000 units, etc.) without declaring whether or not that lot size quantity is feasible, or if there is any capacity to produce that item requested by the supply planning system.

2. **To have more ability to model the constraint and to attach costs to the constraint in the event that cost optimization is used as the supply planning method.** In cost optimization, both fixed and variable costs can be assigned to production. Costs must be assigned to any activity with a cost optimizer if the intent is to have the cost optimizer trade off the activity in question with other activities that are the supply planning recommendations.

Although not all supply planning methods incorporate production and resource constraints, all supply planning methods can incorporate production realities, if not their constraints by using the lot sizing.

Constraint-based Planning in the Application

Having discussed constraints and constraint-based planning from a high level, now is a good time to show how these settings look in an application. In SAP SNP, both the production constraints and the transportation constraints can be either continuous or discrete, as can be seen on both of the following screenshots.

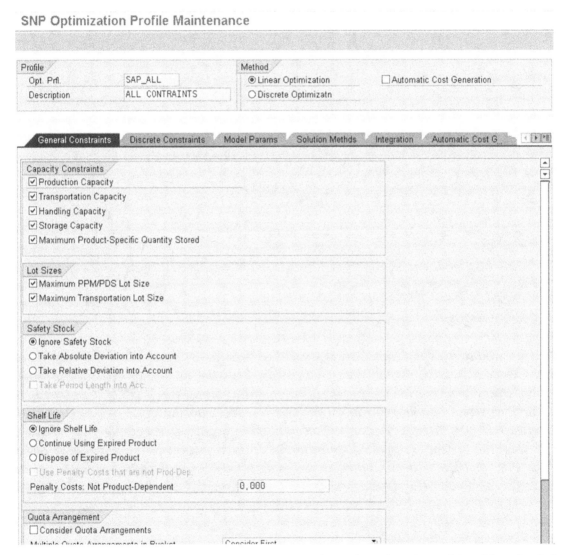

General or linear production constraints are activated or deactivated in this tab of the SNP optimizer.

SNP Optimization Profile Maintenance

Opt. Prfl.	SAP_ALL	⦿ Linear Optimization	☐ Automatic Cost Generation
Description	ALL CONTRAINTS	○ Discrete Optimizatn	

General Constraints | **Discrete Constraints** | Model Params | Solution Methds | Integration | Automatic Cost G

Capacity Constraints

Discrete Production Capacity Increase	0

Lot Sizes

Minimum PPM/PDS Lot Size	0
Integral PPMs/PDS	0
Min. Transportatn Lot Size	0
Integral Transportation Lots	0
Integral Means of Transport	0

Fixed Consumptions

Fixed Material and Resource Consumption	0

Cost Functions

PPM/PDS Execution	0
Means of Transport	0
Procurement Quantity	0

Extended Lot Size Planning

Cross-Period Lot Size	0
Sequence-Dependent Lot Size	0

Discrete production constraints are activated or deactivated in this tab of the SNP opti-mizer. Once activated, the optimizer will incorporate the lot size located in the master data of the system. For instance, activating the Minimum PPM/PDS (PPMs and PDSs are SAP objects that hold routing, BOM, and resource information. To read more about them see this post http://www.scmfocus.com/sapplanning/category/ppm-pds/). Lot Size will cause the system to respect the minimums of the resources that are a subcomponent of the PPM or PDS. The minimum lot sizes can always be in the PPM or PDS, but this tab controls whether the optimizer respects these settings. Each lot size can be different per resource.

Continuous Versus Discrete Optimization

Another important setting with respect to optimization is whether the resources are processed as continuous or discrete. This sounds more complex than it actually is. With both continuous and discrete forms of optimization, the optimizer looks at the resources to determine what is feasible; however, each form of optimization respects the constraints in the resources differently.

Continuous constraining (also known as linear or general) treats the resource capacities as if they can be started and stopped without any batching or lot sizing (for example, a resource could make four units, or 132 units; it would not be limited to batches of fifty, 100, 200, etc.). Setting resources to integer values is another restriction. While it is true that supply planning generally occurs in integers, requiring integer values rather than accepting fractional values and then rounding after the fact makes the optimizer take more time. However, there are few options here because fractions of units don't make very much sense in supply planning.

When constraining in a discrete fashion, decisions are based on the specific capacity stated in the resource. Therefore, if a lot size of fifty is configured in a resource and "discrete" is selected, orders can only be created in quantities of fifty. Optimizing with discrete constraints makes the optimizer look at a greater number of limiting factors and results in a more accurate outcome, and thus a more realistic plan. This overall topic of constraints is a bit complex because both the objective function and the constraints can be either linear or discrete. However, in this case I am referring to the linear or discrete nature of the constraints only.

Lot sizes can be activated for one category of lot sizes or for all of them. Turning on discrete constraints for the optimizer, however, makes the results less optimal (i.e., the objective function cost is higher) and causes the cost optimizer to take longer to solve. I have run into confusion from clients on this topic, so it is worthwhile discussing it further.

Semi-Discrete Constraint Solves

While often described in binary terms (i.e., "on" or "off"), discrete constraints can be enabled partially or completely, meaning that "discrete" can be enabled for some constraints but not for others. When describing discrete constraint optimization on a project, it is a good practice to be unambiguous about which constraints are discrete and which are continuous.

The Challenges of Constraint-based Planning

Just how poorly prepared companies are to perform constraint-based planning correctly is underappreciated. The main difficulty companies have is obtaining and keeping current the constraint data so that the data represents the reality of the constraints in the factory, or supply constraints are being used. There are a number of basic issues concerning constraint data which are listed below:

- Many companies do not maintain adequate databases on the history of work center and resource capacities or their sequence. This information is needed in order to set up the model correctly.

- Few companies are willing to make the effort to constantly update these constraints as things change in the supply chain.

- Resources taken out of commission for scheduled and unscheduled maintenance also need to be reflected in the resources capacity.

- Companies do not become experts at maintaining this type of information quickly, but require a cultural change that is focused on data maintenance. Companies require time to improve both resource and BOM maintenance.

- Companies often rely on spreadsheets for the maintenance of constraint information, but there is specialized software for this that not only does the job better, but also allows more people with necessary information to participate in the process. Even though there are a number of BOM management system/software (BMS) applications, most companies are stuck using antiquated approaches. This means BOM management is still a challenging aspect of supply chain implementations in supply and production planning that rely on this data.

Before a company goes down the path of constraint-based planning, the first question to ask is whether or not the company has any experience maintaining their resource data in such a way that it can be relied upon. Companies may answer this question with "the constraint information will be developed as the project progresses," or "this is a 'change management' issue." Answers such as these can be simply translated into "no it won't." In fact, in my experience, this means the company is not prepared to move to constraint-based planning and would be wasting money on an implementation, hiring and paying for software and consulting before they have the ability to pull the implementation off successfully.

Conclusion

Constraint-based planning restricts activities to declared limits as specified in resources. The system moves loads and locates and relocates capacity automatically during the planning run. Different domains of the supply chain have different types of resources and this fact must be reflected in the model in a way that accounts for unique properties of different resource types. The most common resource constraints to place into a supply planning application are not supply planning constraints but rather production constraints. Constraint-based planning has a number of benefits over unconstrained planning—primarily the fact that it makes a constrained plan with accurately determined resources feasible.

An important distinction between the APS supply planning method of heuristics and the methods of allocation and cost optimization is that the latter two can be performed in a constrained way; however, they can also be used with no constraints. Constraints must both be activated, and kept accurate in order for really constraint-based planning to be performed.

In order to socialize the concepts of constraints, I use a small optimization model with smaller solvers such as Frontline, which can be accessed from Excel. Small optimization models are easier to understand and explain than a big complex enterprise cost optimizer. This approach increases business owners' understanding of constraints, something that needs to happen as the business owners will be responsible for providing the constraint values.

Using either allocation or optimization software allows for the inclusion of constraints that are not restricted to the supply planning domain, such as constraints taken from production planning. Discrete optimization is a more challenging form of optimization that results in more realistic planning output, but also in less optimal or higher cost output. However, the point of any modeling exercise is to make the model as accurate as is reasonable (not as "possible," because increased model accuracy requires more costs, both in the short term and in the long term), not to attain an optimal solution based upon the most simplified assumptions.

Finally, constraint-based planning is challenging and requires a strong commitment to maintaining master data and continual input from the business to keep the constraint information current with the reality of resources in the supply chain.

CHAPTER 4

Resources

Different domains of the supply chain have different types of resources. For instance, trucks are a resource for supply planning, while a work-station is a resource for production planning. However, all resources work similarly in that they have a capacity that can be declared to the planning system. With unconstrained planning (or infinite planning), capacities may or may not be declared, and, if they are declared, there is nothing to stop the system from placing an unlimited load on any resource. With constraint-based planning, three things happen: (1) resources are both declared; (2) at least one of the resources in each process chain has its capacity constrained or capped; (3) the system can only load the resource up to that cap before moving further loads to a different time or to an alternative resource.

Of the different supply and production planning methods available in APO, only prioritization/allocation (CTM) and cost optimization have the ability to run in a constrained fashion. However, this occurs only if the system is configured to manage resources in a finite manner. It is important to understand the distinction between what any system is capable of doing and what it is actually doing in a specific implementation. (This mistake is made in many areas of software evaluation. For instance, it is often stated that an application has a capability of doing something, but this does not say anything about how effective the functionality is or how difficult or easy it is to configure or to maintain.)

The Resource Types

Resources are the mechanism for both constraining the plan in SAP APO and determining if a plan is feasible. Resources apply to SNP, PP/DS, and TP/VS. However, a resource type is the category of the resource, and because different resources do different things, there are different resource types in SAP APO. The most common resources used in SAP APO are production resources, and this applies both to SNP and PP/DS. Therefore, SNP creates the "initial production plan," in addition to creating the initial or network supply plan. Then PP/DS, when deployed (not all companies that implement SNP implement PP/DS, and not all companies that implement SNP implement a production planning and scheduling system—but most do), follows the supply plan and produces a more detailed production plan and finally a production schedule. SNP can plan down to the daily bucket; however, within the day, the supply planning system lacks visibility. When planning occurs for production within the day, this is called scheduling, and is only performed by the DS portion of PP/DS. There are four types of resources in APO that apply to SNP and PP/DS, or to supply planning and production planning. A link to an article is provided below for those interested in more on this topic.

http://www.scmfocus.com/sapplanning/2009/05/02/scm-resource-types/

The following resources are available within APO:

1. *Storage:* Used to model the storage capacity within locations. Storage resources are occasionally used, and I have been asked to activate them on projects. I have also seen several projects where storage resources were capacity-constrained, but in both cases the constraint was deactivated after a brief period because in reality the companies did not want to actually constrain based upon storage capacity. Storage resources cannot be capacity-leveled. Therefore, in the several cases I have seen storage resources used, they have primarily been used for visibility.

2. *Handling (Unit):* A resource is intimately tied to the goods issue (GI) and goods receipt (GR) process. When it is used, it is more as a necessary configuration item to achieve another objective such as using the GR/GI processing time in a particular way. In reality, handling resources are inexpensive and generally not considered strategic. While there are exceptions for specialty products, handling resources consist primarily of things like warehouse workers, forklifts, roller conveyers, etc. More on this is explained at this article link:

http://www.scmfocus.com/sapplanning/2012/12/06/the-goods-receipt-processing-time-and-the-handling-resource/

However, I will later describe how a handling resource can be used to model the overall processing capacity of a location for both inbound and outbound processing.

3. *Transportation:* Transportation resources can be used by either SNP or TP/VS. I don't cover TP/VS in this book and TP/VS has very few implementations globally, even though it is one of the original five APO modules. Furthermore, I have never seen transportation resources used in SNP and there is a good reason for this, which I will describe in more detail later in this chapter.

4. *Production:* This option models production capacity in the factories. These are by far the most used resources in APO. They are not only used in PP/DS, but are also the most commonly used resources in SNP. In fact, I cannot recall an SNP implementation that I either implemented or saw after the fact that did not use production resources.

So now that we have reviewed the different resource types (every resource that is created in APO must be assigned to one of these resource types), we can discuss what these resources represent. Some specific examples of supply chain planning constraints include the following:

- The maximum amount of material that can be placed in a truck
- The maximum amount a bottleneck resource on a production line can produce in an hour
- The maximum number of miles a truck can drive in a day
- The maximum output available from a piece of machinery

- The maximum amount a bin at a warehouse can hold
- The maximum amount of material in total a warehouse can hold
- The time windows (i.e., calendar) that is acceptable for material delivery for production facilities—warehouses and retail locations

The different resource types are apparent in both the resource setup, as well as the Selection Profiles in the planning book when resources are selected.

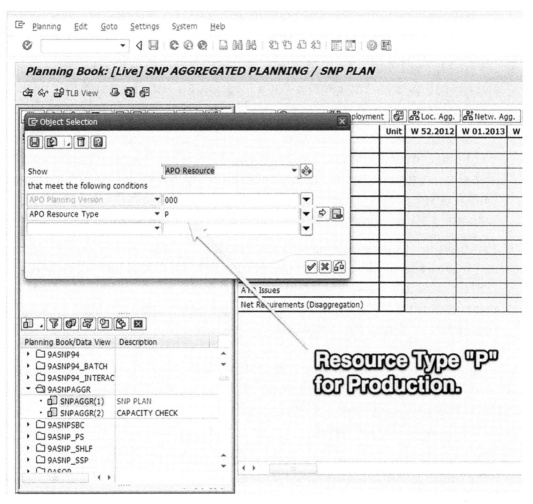

Here in the Selection Profile of the planning book I have defined a resource selection, and then asked to see only "P" for production resources. I can bring up all production resources by doing this.

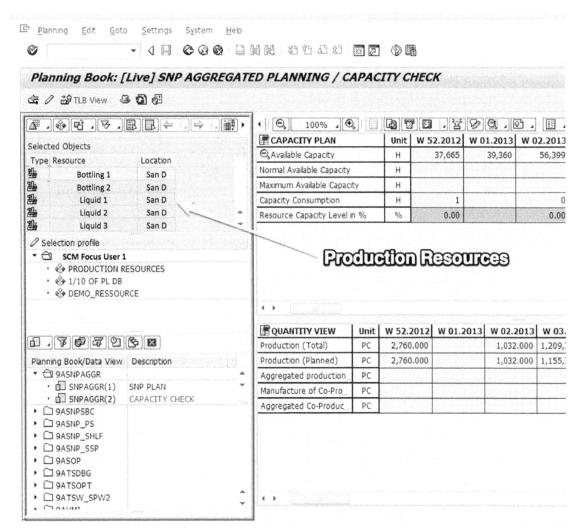

If I select all the production resources and then select the open folder, I can see all scheduled production on all resources. This can also serve as a report, as I can see the total resource utilization in this view.

Production Batch Sizes versus Full Resource Constraints

Supply planning software can represent production planning constraints by using lot sizes on internally-produced products. Doing so would serve to batch production orders for the supply plan when using any of the supply planning methods. A supply planning system could have lot sizing without incorporating any resources into the system. Furthermore, resource constraints, which are of course far more detailed than lot sizes, can also be included when using either the allocation or cost optimization methods. There are two main reasons why production constraints should be included with resource constraints in a supply planning system rather than relying upon production lot sizes:

1. *To Constrain the Plan to a Feasible Schedule:* Production lot sizes simply declare the batch in which an order must be produced (500 units, 1000 units, etc.) without declaring whether or not that lot size quantity is feasible, or if there is any capacity to produce that item requested by the supply planning system.

2. *To Model the Constraint:* This allows the ability to model the constraint and attach costs to the constraint in the event that cost optimization is used as the supply planning method. In cost optimization, both fixed and variable costs can be assigned to production. Costs must be assigned to any activity with a cost optimizer if the intent is to have the cost optimizer trade off the activity in question with other activities that are the supply planning recommendations. Although not all supply planning methods incorporate production and resource constraints, all supply planning methods can incorporate production realities (if not their constraints) by using lot sizing.

The Types of Constraints Commonly Used by Supply Planning Systems

While constraint-based supply planning is discussed frequently, and many software vendors talk about the full complement of resources that they offer, the talk is usually about what software is capable of hypothetically, rather than how it is typically implemented. The various books or vendor manuals on resources would lead one to believe that a wider variety of resources are typically used in supply and production planning than actually are used. Therefore, the most common resources used in supply planning and why they are used are discussed much less frequently.

Constraint-based planning, an approach to planning that has been demonstrated to work well with respect to production resources, does not translate the same way to supply resources. Constraint-based planning actually began in production planning and scheduling, and then migrated into supply planning. However, supply planning and production planning are significantly different. Production planning models a sequence of activities that are implemented by resources. In discrete manufacturing, the activities are usually sequential (one resource completes a process and the next resource begins work on the material). In true process manufacturing (as opposed to mixing operations), the resources are still sequential, but they are lagged and the overall sequence is a good deal more complex than in discrete manufacturing. However, as long as a series of operations is sequential, production planning can be easily throttled or constrained by the resource with the lowest capacity along the line—the so-called bottleneck resource. The sequential and closely interdependent nature of the production line allows it to be effectively constrained by one resource, meaning that it is only necessary to model one resource along the entire line. I learned this rule through my project work, as books tend to describe the theory behind constraint-based supply planning rather than its practical implementation.

How Supply Planning Resources Differ from Production Planning Resources

Unlike production resources, supply planning resources (storage, location, shipping and receiving, and transportation) are not in a direct sequence. When each is used in reality, supply planning resources have substantial lags between them. For instance, stock will often stay in a warehouse for some time before being moved onto a truck and on to the next destination in the supply network. Factories have work-in-process between work stations/resources, and the lag is much less substantial. Rather than being part of a manufacturing process, supply planning is made up of distinct processes. For instance, goods issue, the transportation of products, the goods receipt, and put-away are really separate processes.

Clearly, the requirement of constraining production planning is much easier to meet than the requirement of constraining supply planning resources. Production constraints are also much more prone to being constrained and in fact are more important for a company to constrain than supply planning resources.

Therefore, the most common resources to be constrained in supply planning systems are not supply planning resources, but production resources. Both supply planning and production planning use production resources. SNP creates an initial production plan, which is at a higher level but which looks out considerably further than the PP/DS final production plan and detailed schedule. There are other differences. For instance, SNP will tend to use bucketed resources, while PP/DS will use time continuous resources (configuring mixed resources allows a single resource to be used by both SNP and PP/DS as it has both bucket and time continuous orientation tabs).

APO Resources in Detail

Resources represent the various capacities within both supply and production planning. SNP can use all the resource types (as SNP can use production resources in addition to supply planning resources), while PP/DS can only use production resources. Therefore, instead of covering resources separately in SNP and PP/DS, it made more sense—to me at least—to dedicate a chapter to resources.

Time Settings on the Resource

The following time-related settings can be found for the various resources that can be set up in APO.

- Single
- Single-Mixed
- Multi-Mixed
- Production Line
- Line Mixed* (Only used in IPPE, not frequently used)
- Bucket
- Vehicle* (Only used for TP/VS, so not covered in this book)
- Transportation* (Used in SNP, but infrequently used as transportation is rarely a hard constraint)
- Calendar* (Not frequently used)
- Calendar Mixed* (Not frequently used)

In this chapter I will cover timing-related fields for the resource types just listed, except those with an asterisk next to them.

While each resource has its own set of tabs and time-related fields, most of these fields are identical or similar. Rather than repetitively listing all the timing-related fields for each resource, I will list the similar timing fields for all of the resources, but note where there are differences. Additionally, I will highlight those resources that have timing fields that other resources do not.

First, let's define some of the resources that appear in this chapter and that are integral to understanding the different resources classifications. We will define the following types of resources:

- Bucket versus Time Continuous Resources
- Mixed Resources
- Single versus Multi Resources
- Single-Mixed versus Multi-Mixed Resources

Bucket versus Time Continuous Resources

A bucket resource has a quantity capacity that is planned on a daily basis and would be defined as something like "400 bottles per day." A bucket-oriented resource is based upon a Bucket Oriented Dimension, the options of which are listed here:

- Area
- Density
- Elec. Current
- Energy
- Force
- Frequency
- Length
- Mass

- Mass flow

- Power

- Pressure

- Speed

- Temperature

- Time

- Volume

After you have selected a Bucket Oriented Dimension, you then select the unit of measure for the dimension. This is different than a time-continuous resource, as noted below:

1. *Time Continuous Planning:* This is applied to PP/DS PPMs and PDSs and provides the highest detail available within APO. However, PP/DS can be set up as a bucket capacity, and in this case, it is necessary to set up a Single Mixed resource. The PP/DS Bucket Capacity tab exists on only this time-continuous planning resource type.

2. *Bucket Oriented Planning:* Bucket Oriented Planning uses the SNP PPM or PDS, which is more abstract.

Technically speaking, SNP can use time-continuous resources, in that they can be set up in the system. However, as SNP does not schedule below the day, it makes little sense to have SNP use a time-continuous resource.

This topic is explained further at the following link.

http://www.scmfocus.com/sapplanning/2012/08/19/time-continuous-planning-versus-bucket-in-ctm-and-ppds/

Mixed Resources

The nature of the bucket versus time-continuous resource also relates to the topic of the mixed resource. As I have stated, SNP uses bucketed resources, while PP/DS uses time-continuous resources. However, a mixed resource can be set with both bucketed time master data parameters and time-continuous master data parameters. SAP provides the following, highly illuminating quotation on the topic of mixed resources:

> *If you want to consider the resource loads caused by PP/DS orders in SNP planning, and adjust the SNP planning accordingly, you must use mixed resources (single-mixed resources or multi-mixed resources). In mixed resources, you define the bucket capacity for period-oriented planning in SNP and the time-continuous capacity for time-continuous planning in PP/DS. An SNP order utilizes the bucket capacity of a mixed resource and a PP/DS order utilizes the time-continuous capacity of a mixed resource. For SNP planning, the amount of bucket capacity utilized by PP/DS orders is displayed as an aggregated capacity requirement. SNP planning can therefore take account of the PP/DS orders. For PP/DS planning, the time-continuous capacity used by SNP orders is not displayed. — **SAP Help***

Therefore, a mixed resource has both bucket and time-continuous master data parameters (both for timing—which are discussed here, and also for other settings not covered in this book). A mixed resource can be used for both SNP and PP/DS—that is two different applications, but one resource. However, each application uses the resource—or looks at the resource—in its own way, which helps to explain how production resources that are shared by SNP and PP/DS can be the same. This is a very common question on projects.

Single (Activity) versus Multi (Activity) Resources

After the difference between multi resources and non--multi resources is made clear, there is a distinction between single or mixed resource. A single resource only allows one activity to be performed at one time on the resource, while a multi-resource allows more than one activity to be performed at one time.

Single-mixed or Multi-mixed Resources

Single-mixed and multi-mixed resources work in the following way:

1. *Single-mixed Resource:* This resource can only process one activity at a time, but can be used by both SNP and PP/DS because this resource type has both time-continuous and time-bucketed master data. (Actually, this resource type can be used for time-bucketed planning for both PP/DS and for SNP, or time-continuous planning for PP/DS and timed-bucketed planning for SNP.)

2. *Multi-mixed Resource:* This resource can process multiple activities at a time, but can be used by both SNP and PP/DS because this resource type has both time-continuous and time-bucketed master data. (However, unlike the single mixed resource, this resource can only be used for time-continuous planning for PP/DS.)

Resource Settings and What This Means for Time-Continuous versus Bucket Planning

Different resource types, such as single-mixed and multi-mixed, can be set up to be used by both SNP and PP/DS. However, how the resources are used can change in SNP depending upon the setting. As is highlighted in the quote below, both time-continuous and bucket-oriented planning can use mixed resources.

> *If you want to consider the resource loads caused by PP/DS orders in SNP planning, and adjust the SNP planning accordingly, you must use mixed resources (single-mixed resources or multi-mixed resources). In mixed resources, you define the bucket capacity for period-oriented planning in SNP and the time-continuous capacity for time-continuous planning in PP/DS. An SNP order utilizes the bucket capacity of a mixed resource and a PP/DS order utilizes the time-continuous capacity of a mixed resource. For SNP planning, the amount of bucket capacity utilized by PP/DS orders is displayed as an aggregated capacity requirement. SNP planning can therefore take account of the PP/DS orders. For PP/DS planning, the time-continuous capacity used by SNP orders is not displayed. –**SNP Help***

The system can automatically derive the bucket capacity of a mixed resource from the time-continuous capacity. Since you do not plan with so much detail in SNP (for example, you do not use sequence-dependent setup times), you can reduce the bucket capacity derived using a loss factor. You obtain such a buffer for detailed planning in PP/DS.

For single-activity resources, multi-activity resources, and calendar resources, or for the available time-continuous capacity resources of mixed resources, always enter a rate of resource utilization of 100 percent and a break duration of 00:00:00. Otherwise liveCache determines a different duration than does CTM planning for the corresponding activities. This may cause the system to fulfill the demand too late.

> *CTM always prefers to plan activities overlapping on multi-activity resources and does not support the synchronization of activities. Ensure that the No Synchronization setting in the Resource Master on the Planning Parameters tab page under SyncStart is selected. Otherwise the SAP liveCache executes a synchronization for the corresponding activities. — **SAP Help***

This is shown in the graphic below, which emphasizes and reinforces these points.

Resource Types and Their Function

Function		Single	Single Mixed	Multi	Multi Mixed
	Can Represent Both Time Bucketed and Time Continuous Resources	No	Yes	No	Yes
	Can Perform More than one Operation at a Time	No	No	Yes	Yes
	Can Represent Both Time Bucketed and Time Continuous Resources, as well as Specifically Time Bucketed Resource for both SNP and PP/DS	No	Yes	No	No

Now that we have covered the basic commonly used resource types in APO, we can get into the next layer of detail, which is the timing fields that are on each resource.

Timing Fields Per APO Resource Type

		On Which Tab?	Single	Single Mixed	Multi	Multi Mixed	Production Line	Bucket
Fields	Time Zone	General Data	Yes	Yes	Yes	Yes	Yes	Yes
	Factory Calendar	General Data	Yes	Yes	Yes	Yes	Yes	Yes
	Days +	General Data	Yes	Yes	Yes	Yes	Yes	Yes
	Days 1	General Data	Yes	Yes	Yes	Yes	Yes	Yes
	Start	Time Contin. Capacity	Yes	Yes	Yes	Yes	Yes	No
	End	Time Contin. Capacity	Yes	Yes	Yes	Yes	Yes	No
	Break Duration	Time Contin. Capacity	Yes	Yes	Yes	Yes	Yes	No
	Synchronization Start	Time Contin. Capacity	No	No	Yes	Yes	No	No
	Time Buffer	Time Contin. Capacity	Yes	Yes	Yes	Yes	No	No
	Productive Time in Hours	Time Contin. Capacity	Yes	Yes	Yes	Yes	Yes	No
	{Base Rate} Per	Time Contin. Capacity	No	No	No	No	Yes	No
	Period Type	SNP Bucket Capacity	No	No	No	No	No	Yes
	Number of Periods	SNP Bucket Capacity	No	No	No	No	No	Yes
	{Valid From} Start	Downtimes	Yes	Yes	Yes	Yes	Yes	Yes
	{Valid To} End	Downtimes	Yes	Yes	Yes	Yes	Yes	Yes

As can be seen from the previous matrix, most of the resource types have the same timing fields. The exception here is the bucket resource, which has two timing fields. No other resource type has any of the Time Continuous Capacity fields.

Interestingly, the resources are given the option of either using a set-up matrix or a synchronized start.

Let us evaluate each of the nonproduction constraint types.

Storage Constraints

While it is not the only way to set up a storage constraint, the most common way that I have seen is to set up one storage constraint for the entire location. The unit of measure used for the storage capacity is quite flexible. A location's capacity could be stated in terms of cases that can be accepted by a facility (e.g., 1.5 million cases), or it could be stated in pallet spots. However, in many cases it does not make a lot of sense to have such a high level constraint as the number of cases because the product may need to be in a particular place rather than stored "anywhere." What this means is that a location could be under-capacity regarding the aggregate resource that is stated in cases, but over-capacity for a particular area within the location. It would be necessary to place more storage resources into the system so that the location could be modeled more accurately.

However, it turns out that storage resources are far more "elastic" than production resources. Extra storage is usually available in the form of either third-party warehouses or trailers in the yard. So the total capacity within the four walls is not necessarily limited to the storage capacity at the location's physical building. I have found on several occasions that the actual business requirement vis-à-vis storage resources were the capacity of locations to ship out or receive in certain quantities of product. This would be best modeled with a handling constraint, which I will discuss next. A handling constraint is completely different from a storage constraint at a location.

Handling Resources and Location-to-Location Flow Constraints

If you analyze the constraints related to storage, it is sometimes the case that shipping and receiving are the actual constraints, or what would translate into the handling resource. Locations can only ship and receive a certain amount per day. Without a constraint in place, some days the supply planning system will schedule more volume than the facility can process, meaning that the volume must be pushed manually to the next day.

Setting up a handling resource and constraining the resource for product both arriving and departing from the location can meet this requirement. The maximum amount of product that could be shipped or received in a given day per location would thus be capped. Essentially, a daily aggregate capacity constraint can be accomplished by setting one inbound handling resource to finite and one outbound handling resource to finite.

This is in fact the only scenario—outside of some specialty product—which requires a unique handling resource, where a handling resource for the purposes of constraining capacity would occur. Using a handling resource as described here actually makes a lot of sense, and while I would like to see it implemented, I have yet to see this happen at any company.

Transportation Constraints

For most companies that ship product, transportation constraints for supply planning are not very useful, as most companies can obtain extra transportation capacity when needed. Transportation constraints are different from transportation optimizers for vehicle scheduling. Transportation optimizers are quite useful in optimizing the available time of a truck to get the maximum freight delivered to the most locations. The article below describes a particularly effective and quite inexpensive vehicle scheduling application.

http://www.scmfocus.com/supplychaininnovation/2009/06/google-maps-and-gomobileiq-for-vehicle-routing/

Instead, I am referring to the use of transportation resources in a supply planning application such as SNP. Someone might bring up the topic of private fleets and whether companies that use private fleets may benefit from the use of transportation resources in their supply planning application. It's not that companies don't use private fleets, but in the vast majority of cases, the private fleet is augmented with public for-hire carriers (as is discussed in the article below). Companies that use private fleets one hundred percent of the time, and do not augment their private fleet with outsourced transportation, are exceedingly rare.

http://www.scmfocus.com/fourthpartylogistics/2012/04/the-overestimation-of-outsourced-logistics/

Most companies prefer some carriers over other carriers, and on occasion the preferred carriers are unable to provide capacity. The question is not so much general capacity, but the lead-time between when the request is made for transportation services and when the services can be provided. A good planning system should allow the company to provide adequate lead time on transportation requests, and by placing transportation resources in supply planning applications, a company could get advanced warning when extra external transportation services would be required. But this does not seem to be sufficient incentive to get companies to model their transportation resources.

Resource Uptime

The utilization on the resource can be reduced to equal the average of the change-over time for that resource. This would reduce the capacity of the resource to reflect downtime between changeovers (for SNP).

Therefore, using a period lot size/manufacturing cycle is a more aggregated and less accurate way of keeping manufacturing efficiency high than using a change-over matrix.

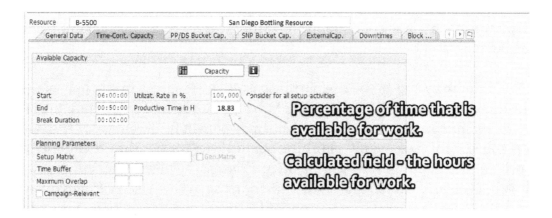

The utilization can be adjusted here in the resource. The utilization adjustment can be used to account for the percentage of time that the resource is not available to do work. The utilization should always be below one hundred percent. Some companies simply take the number of hours that the resource (or production line), was available for work the previous year, and then divide that by the resource's capacity to arrive at a percentage.

BOMs, Routings and Work Centers and the PPM and PDS

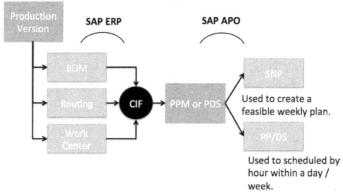

SNP uses the same resources as are used in PP/DS, but in a more aggregated way. What this means is that SNP is "aware" of the same resources that are used in PP/DS. While SNP can use different resources than are used in PP/DS, this is generally not a very good design, and connecting the systems would be higher in maintenance and confusing to manage. Therefore, it is best to use the same production resources in SNP and PP/DS, although resources can be aggregated using the aggregated resource functionality in SNP (although in practice this is done rarely). I do not cover aggregate resource functionality in this book.

Bottleneck Resources in Production Planning

The theory of bottleneck resources is one of the most enduring in production scheduling. I quote from *The Encyclopedia of Operations Management*:

> *Theory of Constraints (TOC)—A management philosophy developed by Dr. Eliyahu M. Goldratt and popularized by his book The Goal, which focuses on the bottleneck resources to improve overall system performance. The TOC recognizes that an organization usually has just one resource that defines its capacity. Goldratt argues that all systems are constrained by one and only one resource. As Goldratt states "a chain is only as strong as its weakest link." This is an application of Pareto's Law to process management and process improvement. TOC concepts are consistent with managerial economics that teach that the setup cost of a bottleneck resource is the opportunity cost of the lost gross margin and that the opportunity cost for a non-bottleneck resource is nearly zero.*

> *According to TOC, the overall performance of a system can be improved when an organization identifies its constraint (the bottleneck) and manages the bottleneck effectively. TOC promotes the following five-step methodology:*

> *1. Identify the System Constraint: Finding the largest queue can often discover the constraint.*

> *2. Exploit the System Constraints: Protect the bottleneck constraint so that no capacity is wasted.*

> *3. Subordinate Everything Else to the System Constraint: Ensure that all other resources (the unconstrained resources) support the system constraint, even if it reduces the efficiency of these resources. For example, unconstrained resources can produce smaller lot sizes so the constrained resource is never starved.*

> *4. Elevate the System Constraints: If this resource is still a constraint, find more capacity. More capacity can be found by working additional hours, using alternate routings, purchasing capital equipment, or subcontracting.*

5. Go Back to Step 1: After a constraint problem is solved, go back to the beginning and start over. This is a continuous process of improvement.

Of course, TOC is a process for improvement. Setting up a bottleneck constraint in an advanced planning application is one particular method or sub-approach of managing the bottleneck resource. Some of the recommendations in the methodology above would occur before the bottleneck is set up in APO. For instance, if a company subcontracts a bottleneck resource, then it may or may not also be entered as a bottleneck resource in SAP APO. That is, the act of subcontracting may mean that the resource is no longer the bottleneck.

It is important to review the theory of constraints, because when SAP was developing SNP and PP/DS it was at least in part copying best-of-breed vendors like i2 Technologies that based their design on TOC. (I have yet to come across any functionality in APO that did not already exist in a best-of-breed vendor.) TOC has died down a bit, but at one time Goldratt's book was extremely influential among manufacturing companies and software vendors that made manufacturing software. Think of the mania surrounding Six Sigma today; that was the popularity level of TOC (roughly speaking) in the 1990s.

Background on Bottleneck Resources

To begin this section, I have included the following definition of a bottleneck resource from Wikipedia:

> *A bottleneck is a phenomenon where the performance or capacity of an entire system is limited by a single or limited number of components or resources. The term bottleneck is taken from the 'assets are water' metaphor. As water is poured out of a bottle, the rate of outflow is limited by the width of the conduit of exit—that is, bottleneck. By increasing the width of the bottleneck one can increase the rate at which the water flows out of the neck at different frequencies. Such limiting components of a system are sometimes referred to as bottleneck points.*

As I described in a previous section, the concept of a bottleneck resource is more applicable to production resources than any of the supply planning resources (storage, handling unit, transportation etc.). The main concept behind bottleneck resources is that the bottleneck is the pacemaker for the entire production line or the entire manufacturing process.

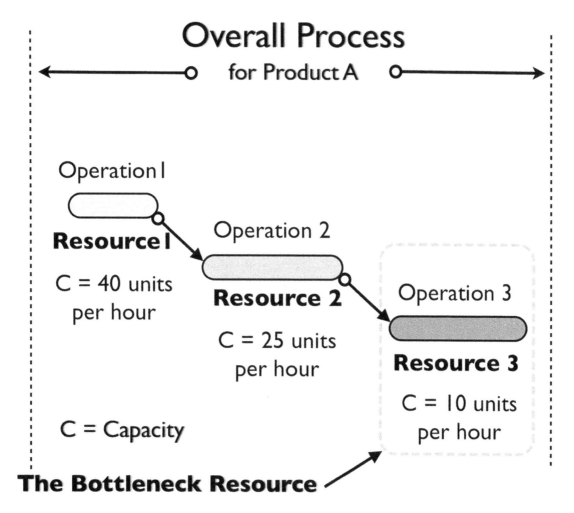

Overall Process
for Product A

Operation 1

Resource 1

C = 40 units per hour

Operation 2

Resource 2

C = 25 units per hour

Operation 3

Resource 3

C = 10 units per hour

C = Capacity

The Bottleneck Resource

The bottleneck operation and resource is Operation Three. Because Resource Three produces the lowest number of units per hour, it restricts the capacity of the overall process, or sequence, to ten units per hour. The overall process cannot exceed the capacity of the slowest resource (unless the slowest resource runs for more hours per day than the rest of the resources). For this reason, it is unnecessary to constrain the capacity of either Resource 1 or Resource 2. This is the standard example and typically applies to a manufacturing problem.

However, while constraint-based planning works better for manufacturing than for supply planning resources, the above scenario works better for ***some manufacturing environments than others***. Very rarely is this fact regarding the match between the application and the environment brought up on projects and especially during sales cycles. Furthermore, some vendors are more limited in the manufacturing environments than they can effectively model. The scenario above works best for discrete manufacturing, where the manufacturing process is a straight "line" with a work center/resource directly transferring an item to the next work center/resource and then directly to the next work center/resource and so on until the production process is complete. It does not work as well when there are leading and lagging operations (for instance, on a product that is incrementally processed), because a lagged operation can process part of the upstream work in progress and is not dependent upon the completion of the previous workstation to begin its work.

There is a strong tendency to over-generalize discrete manufacturing environments to all manufacturing environments, and this over-generalization is not only restricted to software. There are many different manufacturing environments: discrete, process complex, process simple (i.e., mixing operations), repetitive, job shop (i.e., make to order). When permutations are included, the list grows. Nowhere is this overgeneralization more pronounced than in the overemphasis on the Toyota manufacturing system—often referred to as "lean." Toyota's system is a discrete manufacturing system, and therefore its applicability is limited outside of that manufacturing environment.

http://www.scmfocus.com/productionplanningandscheduling/2012/08/25/the-over-generalization-of-discrete-manufacturing-inventory-management/

The book *Production Planning in SAP APO* makes the following point regarding lean manufacturing and the production planning method employed.

This section considers a scenario where there is a bottleneck resource and in which the setup problem is of lesser significance... (this statement describes a manufacturing environment where changeovers are of minimal planning importance) *...the scenarios mapped must not be* *too complex. Such cases are especially widespread in the area of Lean manufacturing. Here the topic of setting up usually plays a secondary role, because planned orders are "long-running" or many similar planned orders are scheduled in a row. In such cases, the mapping of a setup activity is performed, if necessary, by simply blocking the resource using an appropriate dimensionally planned order that is scheduled for a dummy material that has previously been created for this.*

The end of this quotation gets a bit complex and trails off into a solution that is outside of our focus. The interesting thing about the quote is that manufacturing environments, which do not meet the criteria listed above, are frequently the recipient of "Lean manufacturing" initiatives. I have noticed this as well in my consulting work. However, manufacturing environments that are appropriate for Lean manufacturing are specific and can be categorized. Unfortunately, many companies are using Lean-manufacturing principles on environments for which Lean is a poor fit. However, the literature on Lean does not really explain that Lean is designed for specific environments. The way that the literature treats Lean is similar to a pharmaceutical advertisement that makes a drug approved by the Food and Drug Administration for a narrow application appear applicable to the widest possible audience. Most material about Lean proposes that it is a philosophy that applies to every manufacturing environment and also supply planning. There is no attempt to communicate any nuances. For instance, the presentation delivered at ASUG entitled *Enabling Lean Supply Chain Planning* is symptomatic of the material that overgeneralizes and is highly promotional rather than scientifically oriented. Quotes like the following are quite common:

> *Lean principles can have huge returns in reduced inventory carrying cost, scrap and obsolescence.*

Like most promotional literature, there is very little emphasis on the evidence and applicability of an approach, and it is expected that the audience will accept the material uncritically.[7] According to the promotional material, some company somewhere benefitted from the approach at some point in time, so now it's time to do the same thing in your company. Before applicability is established, the typical presentation quickly jumps into the details of how to implement the approach.

Bottleneck Resources in SAP APO

Now that we have covered the definition and etymology of bottleneck resources, we can move on to the topic of the bottleneck resource functionality in SAP APO. There is no direct translation of the general term "bottleneck resource" (as we have just discussed it) to SAP APO. SAP Help states that the following functions apply to a bottleneck resource:

1. *Different Viewing:* On the detailed scheduling planning board (the main user interface for scheduling in PP/DS), bottleneck resources can be displayed differently than non-bottleneck resources.

2. *Separate Campaign Optimization:* In the optimization function of LS>Production Planning and Detailed Scheduling, you can carry out a campaign optimization for bottleneck resources.

The first item shows how the resource is displayed in the interface. The second item shows how the bottleneck resources can be optimized separately from the other resources. However, in both cases this is identification functionality, not any extra functionality that can do something differently with a bottleneck resource that cannot be done to any ordinary finite resource. This is strange because the application definitely gives the impression that it offers some special functionality specific to "bottlenecks."

---

[7] Many of these references to a well-known company are highly suspect. I have now observed several examples of references to a company receiving some extraordinary benefit by implementing some supply chain planning approach, only to have worked in that company and found that they did not do what they were referenced to have done. Many consulting companies simply make up stories about benefits that never happened. Simply having the actual client co-present at a conference with the consulting company is not evidence that the story occurred as they said it did. I have worked on projects where the client had yet to see the benefits proposed by the consulting firm, and where the client was quite unhappy with the performance of the approach and the consulting company. Yet the client representatives still attended the conference with their consulting company and put on a brave face. I have found that companies have the same incentive to appear successful as the consulting companies have in presenting what are often illusory success stories.

It bears mentioning that bottleneck resource functionality is entirely in PP/DS and does not extend to SNP; without PP/DS this functionality cannot be used. SNP creates an initial supply and production plan—which is not aware of the bottleneck designation in the resource that is applied in PP/DS. APO then requires that PP/DS perform its own optimization on bottleneck resources—which is likely to change the initial supply plan created by SNP—and then send this back to SNP. The optimizer screen shows where this is set up.

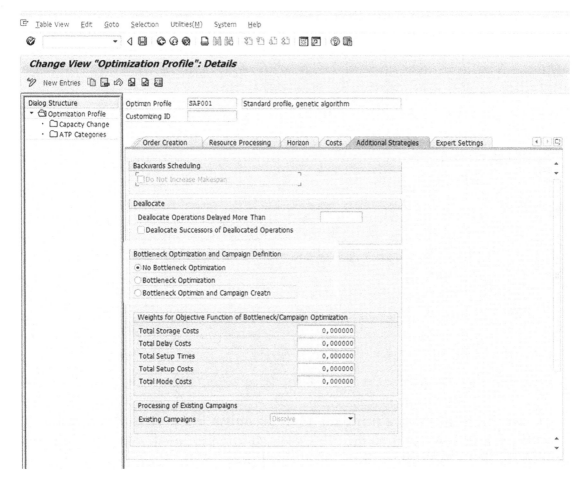

The PP/DS optimizer has the option of paying no attention to the bottleneck setting on the resource, or of constraining all bottleneck resources.

How a bottleneck resource is integrated with infinite resources is an interesting topic, but one which can be difficult to get a solid grasp on.

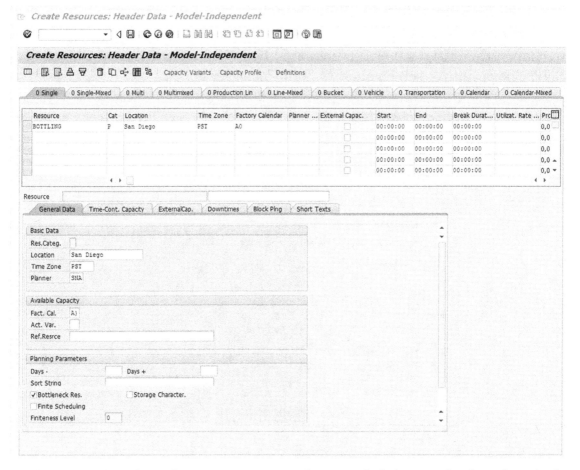

As the screen shot above shows, a resource can be set as infinite, or a bottleneck, or both.

While using a resource in a finite manner has only a few prerequisites (the finite toggle switch on the resource must be selected and the constraint-based method used must be set to finite), using a bottleneck resource is more involved.

Therefore, APO's bottleneck functionality can really be described as "identification functionality." By setting the bottleneck flag on the resource, it can be viewed and can be made part of a campaign optimization. While I have not seen this used on a project, according to the book *Production Planning in SAP APO*, this is commonly employed in the chemical and pharmaceutical industries.

However, SAP's bottleneck functionality and description is inconsistent with the actual definition of a bottleneck resource. A company performs bottleneck resource planning if they take the following steps:

1. The bottleneck resource setting is not checked for any resource.

2. The finite setting is set for a single resource on a production line.

3. The CTM or the SNP or PP/DS Optimizer is run.

If the company also decides to set the bottleneck setting for some or all of the finite resources, then they will be able to identify them and perform a special optimization for them—but this should simply be considered extra functionality. The resource actually becomes the bottleneck resource—or co-bottleneck resource—once the finite setting is selected on the resource.

When Multiple Resources Along a Production Line Must be Modeled

When a manufacturing process is sequential and straightforward to model, it can be finitely planned on the basis of the bottleneck resource. In that circumstance, selecting the right resource to set as the bottleneck resource is simple.

The Production and Resource Scenarios

In this section I will show a variety of production requirements that companies face in real life. The first few scenarios are included to explain the basics of how the resources work in APO, and are too simple to represent real life scenarios. However, as we move through the different scenarios, they will become more and more complex and realistic. With each new scenario we will touch on issues that companies face in modeling their production resources, and we will discuss modeling approaches for addressing these requirements.

Most often many resources are involved in a production process. However, I model only two resources in these examples because I can explain what I need to with just two resources, making it is easier for the reader to follow. In general, production planning does not focus attention onto every resource along a production process, but to just one or two resources. However, I will show in a few of these scenarios that constraining one resource would be insufficient to model the overall production line. Below each graphic I have included the salient features of the scenario.

1. Sequential Resource Constraints

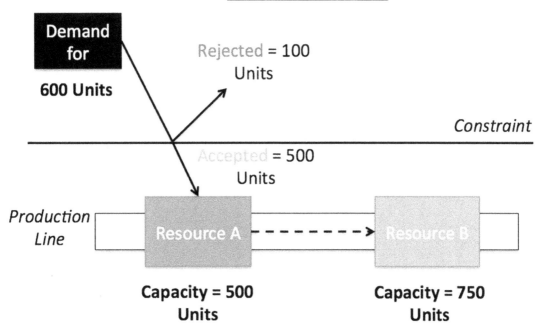

Salient Scenario Features

1. *Finite Resource?—**A***

2. *Resources Feeding or Being Fed by Multiple Resources?—**No***

3. *Different Capacity Per Product Per Resource?*—**No**

4. *Could Some of the Resources be Aggregated?*—**N/A**

5. *Aggregation Reason?*—**N/A**

This is the simplest possible design. The graphic simply explains that if a resource is set as finite, then it restricts the demand that can be accepted/scheduled for the entire production line. That single resource restricts the capacity for the entire production line, and it does not matter if the resource is the first or the last in the production sequence. Also, "rejected" is a general term to mean "not accepted at that period." Automatic capacity leveling that is part of constraint-based planning will attempt to move the demand forward or backward (depending upon the backward and forward scheduling configuration).[8]

The larger capacity of resource B is immaterial to the production rate of this line because the bottleneck resource and where the constraint is placed—resource A—is the pace-setter, and restricts the quantity that can be produced to 500 units. The extra 250 unit capacity of resource B simply goes to waste.

I sometimes get questions about what happens if the resources are set to different units of measure. For instance, in beverage production, the liquid processing resource is measured in gallons per hour, while the bottling resource is measured in bottles per hour, and the final demand is in bottles per hour.

However, this does not mean that the bottleneck resource needs to be set at the bottling resource, if the liquid processing resource is actually the bottleneck. APO will convert all of the capacities and units of measure between the resources. Imagine the following scenario which illustrates how this works:

---

[8] I include forward and backward scheduling in my book *Planning Horizons, Calendars and Timing in SAP APO*. The book compares and contrasts forward and backward scheduling with forward and backward forecast consumption—two areas of functionality that can be easy to confuse with one another.

2. Different Units of Measure Per Resource

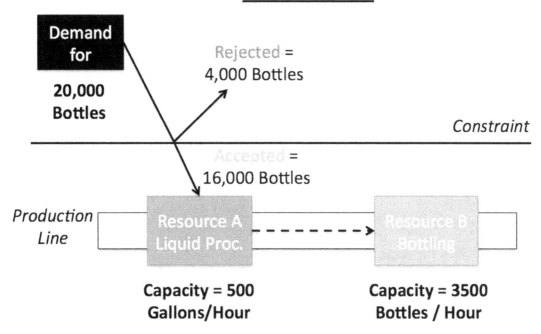

Demand for

20,000 Bottles

Rejected = 4,000 Bottles

Constraint

Accepted = 16,000 Bottles

Production Line

Resource A Liquid Proc.

Resource B Bottling

Capacity = 500 Gallons/Hour

Capacity = 3500 Bottles / Hour

*Available Time for Processing = 8 Hours

Salient Scenario Features

1. *Finite Resource?—**A***

2. *Resources Feeding or Being Fed by Multiple Resources?—**No***

3. *Different Capacity Per Product Per Resource?—**No***

4. *Could Some of the Resources be Aggregated?—**No***

5. *Aggregation Reason?—**N/A***

How does the system know that it should reject 4,000 bottles and accept and create a planned order for 16,000 bottles? One of the functions of the planning system is that it does all of the math that I have listed above automatically. This second scenario is very similar to the first, except that it adjusts for different units of measure between the liquid processing resource and the bottling resource. SAP APO converts the units of measure across a series of resources on a production line. This is standard within the product, and as long as the master data for the product and the resource is set up accurately, APO will perform all of the conversion mathematics. All the company has to do is enter accurate master data and the system will manage the rest.

Constraint Based Planning Math

Requirement	Units
Demand in Bottles	20,000
Resource Capacity in Gallons Per Hour	500
Available Hours on Liquid Processing Resource	8
Resource Capacity in 8 Hours in Gallons	4,000
Number of Bottles Per Gallon	4
Gallons in Bottles That Can be Produced in the Available Time on the Liquid Processing Resource	16,000
Demand That Can be Accepted and Planned	16,000
Demand That Must be Rejected to Moved to a New Period	4,000

Although the ability to perform all of the unit of measure conversion mathematics is infrequently discussed (probably because it is seen as basic functionality), it is a major productivity enhancement with supply planning and production planning systems. Imagine performing these calculations by hand, the potential errors that could ensue, and the costs of those errors? It was not that long ago that all production planning unit of measure conversions were calculated this way.[9]

---

[9] Collectively, we don't spend much time studying the history of supply chain planning. Most works of history instead focus on politics, personalities, and warfare with very light coverage given to the much less glamorous aspects of human activity. I have searched and have been unable to find books (not more than a few actually) or universities that concentrate on this topic. However, it is interesting to learn how things were done in all aspects of supply chain planning, particularly prior to computerization. I have learned a great deal by studying this area, and in particular how incorrect many projections are from those who were ostensibly "experts" in this area. I was always suspicious of the claim that Henry Ford invented the assembly line (in truth, outside of MBA courses, historians only credit him with the automation of the assembly line rather than its actual invention). However the first assembly line for which I could find evidence was The Venetian Arsenal, which built ships for the Venetian city-state over a thousand years ago and was in continual operation for eight hundred years. This topic is covered in the following article: http://www.scmfocus.com/productionplanningandscheduling/2012/07/04/who-was-the-first-to-engage-in-mass-production-ford-or-the-venetians/

http://www.scmfocus.com/scmhistory/

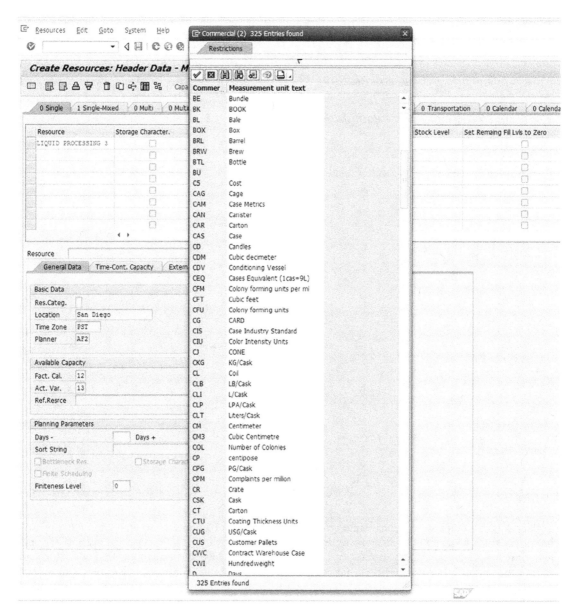

The resources in APO can support an enormous number of units of measure as can be seen from this screen shot. This drop down shows the three hundred and twenty-five measurement units that are available to choose from.

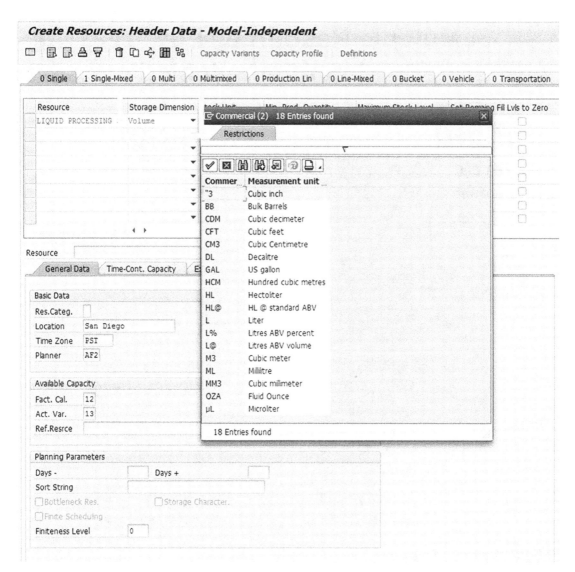

However, the "storage dimension" which can be seen in the screen shot above categorizes the units of measure. Once a storage dimension is selected, the stock units that can be selected are restricted to those that are valid for the storage dimension. In this case, because volume was selected as the storage dimension, the stock units are now restricted to just 18.

3. Multiple Resources Per Area: Not Interchangeable

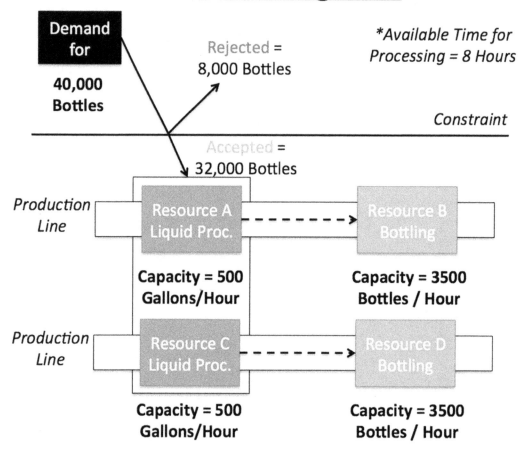

Salient Scenario Features

1. *Finite Resource?—**A, C***

2. *Resources Feeding or Being Fed by Multiple Resources?—**No***

3. *Different Capacity Per Product Per Resource?—**No***

4. *Could Some of the Resources be Aggregated?—**No***

5. *Aggregation Reason?—**N/A***

With this scenario we begin to get a bit more realistic. We have two parallel production lines. They have the same capacity per resource, and they do not differ in rates per product mix. So nothing much has changed from the previous scenario except that we have two production lines instead of one. Due to the physical setup of the plant, resource A can only feed resource B, and resource C can only feed resource D.

This example would be a prime example of an opportunity for resource aggregation. Resources need only be treated as separate if they differ in some way. If not, resources can and should be combined or aggregated. This is different from the aggregated resource functionality in SNP.

4. Multiple Resources Per Area: Interchangeable: Same Capacity Per Product Per Resource

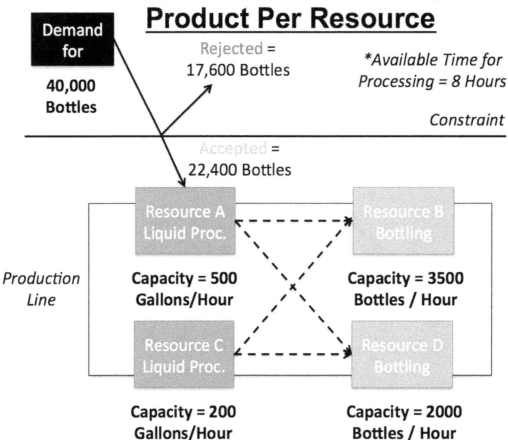

Demand for

40,000 Bottles

Rejected = 17,600 Bottles

Available Time for Processing = 8 Hours

Constraint

Accepted = 22,400 Bottles

Production Line

Resource A Liquid Proc.

Capacity = 500 Gallons/Hour

Resource B Bottling

Capacity = 3500 Bottles / Hour

Resource C Liquid Proc.

Capacity = 200 Gallons/Hour

Resource D Bottling

Capacity = 2000 Bottles / Hour

Salient Scenario Features

1. *Finite Resource?—**A, C***

2. *Resources Feeding or Being Fed by Multiple Resources?—**Yes***

3. *Different Capacity Per Product Per Resource?—**No***

4. *Could Some of the Resources be Aggregated?—**Yes (A & C), (B & D)***

5. *Aggregation Reason?—**Both A & C and B & D could be aggregated because they do the same processing and do not differ in their rates based upon products processed. Also, the resources are now interchangeable.***

Several changes dramatically alter this scenario from the previous scenario. First, resources A and C can now both feed resources B or D. Any product can be processed through any resource, enabling the two separate production lines to be treated as one large production line.

A second change from the previous scenario is that the capacities of the liquid resources (A & C) and the bottling resources (B & D) are no longer the same. However, this is not material to whether the resources can be aggregated. Resource AC would be set up in the system with a capacity of 700 gallons per hour and resource BD would be set up with a capacity of 5500 bottles per hour.

Multiple Resource Constraints

Up to this point the scenarios have focused only on the first resource, the liquid processing resource, as being a constraint to the production process. In the following scenarios we will add an extra complexity, which is based upon the effect on capacity of changing the product mix. Here the capacity of the bottling line changes depending upon which product is to be bottled. This scenario is actually very easy to visualize. Simply increasing the size of the bottle would tend to increase the capacity of the bottling operations, because larger bottles have a smaller relative time in motion through the bottling resource versus the volume of liquid processed. Having worked for several beverage companies, I can say that in practice there are quite a few reasons as to why a bottling line capacity could increase per product being processed. However, let's focus on bottle size as that is the easiest to understand. What this means is that if we apply the same modeling that we have up to this point, one particular product mix (which would have larger bottles) would make the liquid processing resource the constraint. However, in other situations, with a different product mix that has smaller bottles, the bottleneck resource would become the bottling resource (no pun intended).

So how can this scenario be properly modeled? One might say that both resources could be set to finite or constrained. However, would that work? Multi-constrained resources can be set for a production process. Therefore the optimization must respect both the liquid constraint and the bottling constraint. So if the bottling constraint is reached before the liquid constraint (because the liquid capacity is higher than the bottling constraint), the optimization must create a planned order for what can be processed at the bottling constraint only, even though there is excess capacity on the liquid constraint. Multiple finite resource planning is standard functionality in both SNP and PP/DS. The book *Production Planning in SAP APO* states it the following way:

> *You can use the PP/DS Optimizer to take several bottlenecks into account at the same time, order priorities can be included, and a multilevel optimization is possible. Because the PP/DS Optimizer does not create or delete any orders, but merely reschedules them, a previous requirements planning is a prerequisite for using the PP/DS Optimizer.*

5a1. Multiple Resources Per Area: Interchangeable: Same Capacity for All Products / Liquid and Bottling Constraints

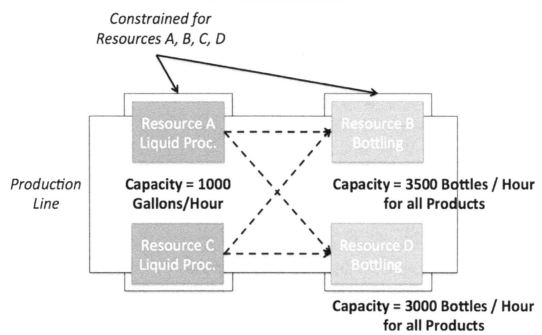

Salient Scenario Features

1. *Finite Resource?—**A-C, B-D***

2. *Resources Feeding or Being Fed by Multiple Resources?—**Yes***

3. *Different Capacity Per Product Per Resource?—**No***

4. *Could Some of the Resources be Aggregated?—**Yes (A & C), (B & D)***

5. *Aggregation Reason?—**Both A & C and B & D could be aggregated because they do the same processing and do not differ in their rates based upon products processed. Also, the resources are now interchangeable.***

This scenario differs from scenario 4 because of the dual constraint, with the bottling resource being an additional constraint; prior to this scenario, only liquid has been a constraint.

5a2. Multiple Resources Per Area: Interchangeable: Different Capacity for All Products / Liquid and Bottling Constraints

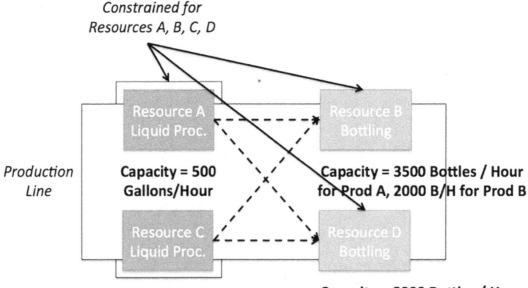

Salient Scenario Features

1. *Finite Resource?—**A–C, B, D***

2. *Resources Feeding or Being Fed by Multiple Resources?—**Yes***

3. *Different Capacity Per Product Per Resource?—**Yes (for B & D only)***

4. *Could Some of the Resources be Aggregated?—**Yes (A & C)***

5. *Aggregation Reason?—**Resource A & C could be aggregated because they do the same processing and do not differ in their rates based upon products processed. But resource B & D could not.***

The difference between this scenario and scenario 5a1 is that there are now different capacities on the bottling line depending upon the product mix (in this case bigger bottles versus smaller bottles).

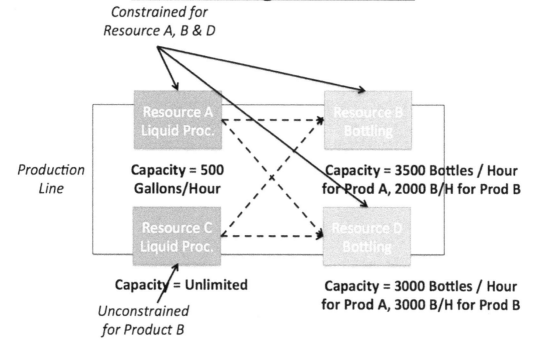

5b. Multiple Resources Per Area: Interchangeable: Different Capacity for All Products / One Liquid and Two Bottling Constraints

Constrained for
Resource A, B & D

Resource A
Liquid Proc.

Resource B
Bottling

Production
Line

Capacity = 500
Gallons/Hour

Capacity = 3500 Bottles / Hour
for Prod A, 2000 B/H for Prod B

Resource C
Liquid Proc.

Resource D
Bottling

Capacity = Unlimited

Unconstrained
for Product B

Capacity = 3000 Bottles / Hour
for Prod A, 3000 B/H for Prod B

Salient Scenario Features

1. *Finite Resource?—**A, B, D***

2. *Resources Feeding or Being Fed by Multiple Resources?—**Yes***

3. *Different Capacity Per Product Per Resource?*—**Yes (for B & D only)**

4. *Could Some of the Resources be Aggregated?*—**No**

5. *Aggregation Reason?*—**Resources cannot be aggregated because of different capacities per resources per product, and because one liquid resource is unconstrained (because it has unlimited capacity for product B, while the other bottling resource is constrained.**

The difference between this scenario and scenario 5a2 is that one liquid resource is unconstrained for one product. The other resource is constrained for all products. (We only assign product B to the unconstrained resource C, and C is not assigned to resource A.)

Hard versus Soft Constraints

In one dimension any optimizer can treat constraints in different ways. There are two extreme forms of constraints, which also happen to be the two most commonly used resource types: hard constraints and soft constraints. Resources are an example of a hard constraint; the optimizer may not exceed or "violate" this type of constraint under any circumstance. Hard constraints make a lot of sense because a production resource that can produce one thousand units per day cannot be made to exceed that production rate without incurring substantially more costs. Hard constraints do not require costs to be associated with them because there is no option to exceed their stated capacities. Things such as transportation costs are not constraints; these costs simply scale with the transportation units scheduled. However, there can be transportation resources, and the transportation resource capacity cannot be exceeded when they are used in their default mode of hard constraint.

A constraint may also be treated as soft; here the constraint may be violated, but at a cost—most often referred to as a penalty or penalty cost. Two of the most important penalty costs/soft constraints in SNP are the penalty cost for violating the safety stock target and the non-delivery penalty cost (or the activity of failing to meet a demand). To see how the safety stock penalty works, here is an example: If a safety stock target is 10 units, and the company holds only 8 units for one planning bucket, the optimizer incurs 10-8 = 2, which is The Penalty Cost for that planning bucket. The safety stock penalty cost is incurred in every bucket for which the safety stock target is violated.

Some costs, such as storage costs or transportation costs, are positive costs in that the optimizer incurs them at the time of activity. Penalty costs are negative costs, and are incurred when the optimizer fails to do something that is desirable. The same dynamic applies for storage costs. In SNP, storage costs are incurred on a daily basis per unit. Another example of a soft constraint is the cost of unfulfilled demand. The objective function of SNP is to minimize costs, so the unfulfilled demand is declared as a penalty cost to encourage or direct the optimizer to meet as many demands as is feasible, given the hard constraints.

Soft constraints were one of the important conceptual developments in optimization, because they allowed the introduction of implicit costs into the model. While not often discussed, soft constraints are interesting because they allow the combination of explicit (or "real") costs along with "implicit" costs, which are essentially imaginary. Luckily for those of us working in supply chain planning optimization, imaginary costs have been extremely well-developed as a concept and explained in the field of economics where they are under the category of "opportunity costs." Wikipedia describes opportunity costs as follows:

> *Opportunity cost is the cost of any activity measured in terms of the value of the next best alternative forgone (that is not chosen). It is the sacrifice related to the second best choice available to someone, or group, who has picked among several mutually exclusive choices. The opportunity cost is also the "cost" (as a lost benefit) of the forgone products after making a choice. Opportunity cost is a key concept in economics, and has been described as expressing "the basic relationship between scarcity and choice." The notion of opportunity cost plays a crucial part in ensuring that scarce resources are used efficiently.*

Imagine my surprise when I found that the opportunity cost entry in Wikipedia had a full explanation of implicit and explicit costs.

Explicit Costs

Explicit costs are opportunity costs that involve direct monetary payment by producers. The opportunity cost of the factors of production not already owned by a producer is the price that the producer has to pay for them. For instance, a firm spends $100 on electrical power consumed; their opportunity cost is $100. The firm has sacrificed $100, which could have been spent on other factors of production.

Examples of explicit costs in SNP include storage costs and transportation costs.

Implicit Costs

Implicit costs are the opportunity costs in factors of production that a producer already owns. They are equivalent to what the factors could earn for the firm in alternative uses, either operated within the firm or rented out to other firms. For example, a firm pays $300 a month all year for rent on a warehouse that only holds product for six months each year. The firm could rent the warehouse out for the unused six months, at any price (assuming a year-long lease requirement), and that would be the cost that could be spent on other factors of production.

Examples in SNP of implicit costs include non-delivery penalty costs and safety stock penalty costs.

More on safety stock penalty costs can be found in the following article.

http://www.scmfocus.com/sapplanning/2011/11/05/how-soft-constraints-work-with-soft-constraints-days-supply-and-safety-stock-penalty-costs/

Finiteness Level of Resources

Resources can be set as finite or infinite for different applications. The settings for doing this can be found both in the method used (with CTM and the PP/DS and SNP Optimizer), as well as on the resource itself. In APO this is referred to as the "finiteness level."

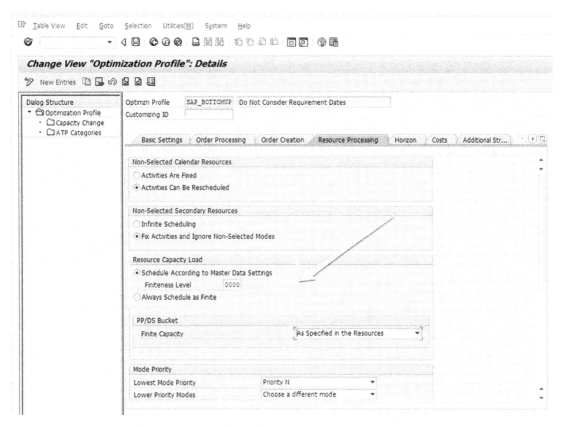

Here we can see the finiteness level setting on the PP/DS Optimizer Profile. In order to know how soft or hard to treat the constraint, the finiteness level must be declared.

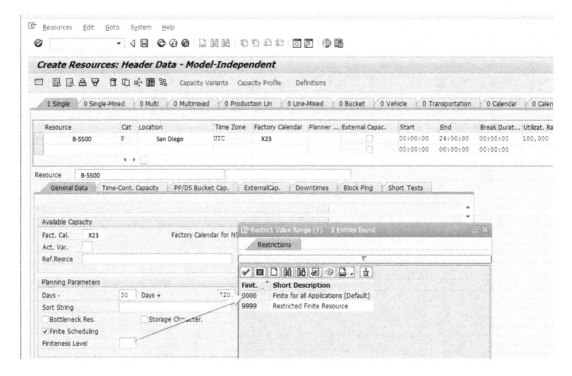

SAP defines the finiteness level of the resource as follows:

> *If the resource is used by several applications, you can use the finiteness level to define which application schedules the resource finitely and which schedules infinitely. If you do not assign any finiteness level to the resource, the default value is 0. The maximum possible value is **9999**. If you enter this value, only the applications in which the finiteness level is also **9999** schedule the resource finitely. If you enter the value 0, all applications in which finite scheduling is set schedule these resources finitely, irrespective of the finiteness level defined there.*

Finiteness level	Short description
0	*Finite for all applications (default)*
100	*For PP finite resource*
200	*For DS finite resource*
300	*For PP/DS optimization finite resource*
9999	*Restricted finite resource*

In PP the resource should be scheduled infinitely, and in DS it should be scheduled finitely. You enter the finiteness level 200 at the resource R1. In the PP strategy profile, you define that only resources with a finiteness level smaller than or equal to 100 should be scheduled finitely. In the DS strategy profile, you enter 200 for this value. PP therefore schedules infinitely on R1, while DS schedules finitely.

Conclusion

Different domains of the supply chain have different types of resources that must be modeled. For instance, trucks are a resource for supply planning, while a work-station is a resource for production planning. Of the different supply and production planning methods available in APO, only prioritization/allocation (CTM) and cost optimization have the ability to run in a constrained fashion. However, this occurs only if the system is configured to manage resources in a finite manner.

Resources are the mechanism for both constraining the plan in SAP APO and determining if a plan is feasible. Placing resources into a supply planning system is the next step up from using simple lot sizes in the emulation of production constraints. Because of the nature of some manufacturing processes and the fact that they are often sequential, constraint-based applications for production planning leverage this fact into modeling only the bottleneck resource. However, supply planning resources and supply planning in general are less sequential in nature, and some resources (e.g., transportation resources or handling resources) are not constrained in the same manner as production resources. For instance, tendering freight to external providers can easily attain transportation resources. Handling resources are inexpensive and can be easily added. Storage resources, or the capacity in a warehouse, may seem like a hard constraint, but material may be held in trailers outside the facility, or the company may take advantage of third-party warehouses in the case of overflow. Production resources are more valuable to model and to constrain than supply planning resources, as is evidenced by the fact that the most common resources modeled in both supply planning and production planning applications are production resources.

Resources represent the various capacities within both supply and production planning. SNP can use all the resource types (SNP can use production resources in addition to supply planning resources), while PP/DS can only use production resources.

This chapter covered the timing-related fields for resources. With the exception of the bucket resource, most of the timing-related fields across the commonly used resource types are identical. Where they differ is in how the resource is used by APO—whether the resource is a production, handling, storage, or transportation resource. Of the commonly used resource types, the most important distinction between them is the following characteristics:

- Bucket versus Time Continuous

- Mixed versus Non Mixed

- Single (Activity) versus Multi (Activity)

It is the mixed resources that can be used both by SNP and PP/DS, because they contain both timing-related fields for bucket-oriented and time-continuous planning. The most commonly used resources in APO are essentially named as one combination of the characteristics listed above. However, in addition to the resource timings, the method that interacts with these resources can be designed to work in different ways. For instance, CTM—traditionally a supply planning method that works in bucket-oriented planning and generates SNP planned orders—can also be set to time-continuous planning and to generate PP/DS planned orders.

As with a location, a calendar can have a resource associated with it that determines the workdays of the resource. The resource-available times, which are declared within each resource, then operate within the open days of the calendar. A resource is populated with a capacity, which can be constrained or unconstrained, but the location calendar, resource calendar and the start, end, and break duration form another constraint that is as important as the capacity value assigned to the resource.

The resource calendars control when the resource is available for work. First the factory and distribution calendars are set up, and then they are assigned to resources and to planning calendars. The holiday calendar is in turn assigned to the factory and distribution center calendar. Both the holiday calendar and the factory calendar are created using the same screen.

This chapter covered the original theory of bottleneck resources and also how SAP defines "bottleneck" resources. As with many areas of SAP functionality, it turns out that SAP's definition is not the same as the generally accepted definition. The bottleneck functionality in APO is really more about identification and segmentation of resources for special treatment than it is about meeting the classical definition of a bottleneck.

Included in this chapter were a number of scenarios that moved from the most simple to the most complex, and involved the use of two sets of sequential resources: liquid resources and bottling resources. These scenarios showed us how the characteristics of the resources allow them to be set up differently depending upon how the resources process product.

Resources fall into the category of "hard" constraints. Hard constraints cannot be violated at any cost. A second category of constraints—soft constraints—may be violated at a cost. These costs are modeled as penalty costs, which are negative costs incurred when the optimizer fails to do something which would be desirable from the business perspective for the optimizer to do. Soft constraints are interesting because they allow the combination of explicit—or "real"—costs along with "implicit" costs, which are, in a way, imaginary.

In APO a constraint can be set to different levels of "finiteness," which means that the resource can be finite for some applications but infinite for others.

CHAPTER 5

Forecast Consumption, Allocation, Scheduling Direction and Timings

An important consideration regarding capacity leveling are the settings that place the demand upon the supply elements. The settings in this chapter will explained these settings. In this chapter, I cover several settings that are similar in that they can be set backward or forward. Their brief definitions are included below:

1. *Forecast Consumption:* How the sales orders consume or reduce the forecast.

2. *Allocation Consumption:* How the sales orders consume allocations.

3. *Scheduling Direction:* How planned production orders and purchase requisitions are scheduled forward and backward in time from the day on which they would be scheduled given optimal circumstances.

We will start with backward and forward forecast consumption.

Backward and Forward Forecast Consumption

Backward forecast consumption means that current sales orders can go backward as many days as the system is configured in order to consume the forecast. Forward forecast consumption means the current sales orders can go forward as many days as the system is set in order to consume the forecast. The forecasts for prior periods are being applied to future periods, allowing the remainder of unconsumed forecast quantities to be consumed by periods of high sales orders. Forecast consumption occurs in SNP, and is set in the Requirements Strategy sub-tab of the Demand tab of the Product Location Master.

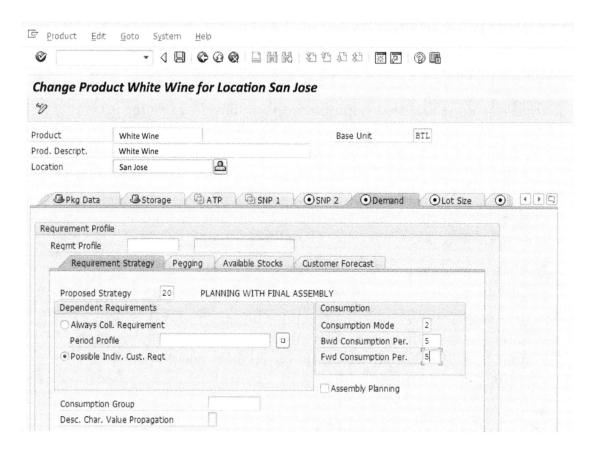

The fields on this screen are as follows:

1. *Consumption Mode: Controls the direction on the time axis in which the system consumes the forecast (Options are: Backward consumption, Backward/forward consumption, Forward consumption).*

2. *Backward Consumption Period: Defines the consumption period (in calendar days) for backward consumption. The consumption period is in calendar days not workdays. Since SNP and PP/DS can use different calendars, it is not possible to define a calendar for use with consumption. This may lead to unexpected results.*

3. *Forward Consumption Period: Defines the consumption period (in calendar days) for forward consumption.*

The Example

The mockup of the SAP Planning Book and its logic shown on the following page provide an example of where forecast consumption induces over-ordering. The overall orders that would be generated are compared both with and without backward consumption. The key figures without backward consumption are highlighted in light pink.

	Initial (Past 5 Calendar Days)	Monday	Tuesday	Wednesday	Thursday	Friday	Totals
Actual Forecast	*6,000*	*2,000*	*2,000*	*2,000*	*2,000*	*2,000*	*10,000*
Forecast (*unconsumed forecast*) - with 5 day backward consumption		-	-	-	-	500	*500*
Forecast (*unconsumed forecast*) - with no backward consumption	1,000	500	500	-	-	500	*2,500*
Sales Orders		1,500	1,500	5,000	3,200	1,500	*12,700*
Production or procurement orders with backward consumption		1,500	1,500	5,000	3,200	2,000	*13,200*
Production or procurement orders with no backward consumption		2,000	2,000	5,000	3,200	2,000	*14,200*

Here we can see that the sales order of 5,000 units consumes unconsumed forecast from the previous periods. This adjusts the production or procurement orders down for Monday and Tuesday and may have also reduced the production or procurement orders from the initial column, depending upon when the sales order was recorded in the system. Secondly, the total order quantity with five-day backward consumption is closer to the actual demand for that period.

	Initial (Past 5 Calendar Days)	Monday	Tuesday	Wednesday	Thursday	Friday	Totals
Actual Forecast	*6,000*	*2,000*	*2,000*	*2,000*	*2,000*	*2,000*	*10,000*
Forecast (*unconsumed forecast*) - with 5 day backward consumption		-	-	-	-	500	500
Forecast (*unconsumed forecast*) - with no backward consumption	1,000	500	500	-	-	500	2,500
Sales Orders		1,500	1,500	5,000	3,200	1,500	12,700
Production or procurement orders with backward consumption		1,500	1,500	5,000	3,200	2,000	13,200 vs.
Production or procurement orders with no backward consumption		2,000	2,000	5,000	3,200	2,000	14,200

Forecasts have effectively been "pushed forward" to where they are consumed by sales orders. Using neither backward nor forward consumption promotes an upward bias in ordering. With backward consumption enabled, the total demand is closer to the actual demand. Without the ability to consume from other periods, the high sales orders on Wednesday will convert to production or procurement orders, but previous periods where the forecast was higher are not reduced.

One additional outcome of the backward consumption displayed above was to push the ordering forward to match sales orders rather than to match the forecast. While this outcome is not discussed often, it is beneficial. When forward forecast consumption is enabled, future ordering based purely on forecasts is reduced; however, only backward consumption postpones the orders generated to better align with sales orders.

Now that we have covered how forecast consumption works and its benefits, let's delve into some interesting questions regarding forecast consumption.

Implications to the Question of Backward Forecast Consumption

Here are some questions that should be discussed when explaining forecast consumption:

1. What is the purpose of forecast consumption in the same period? (In fact, one can set the forecast consumption to have zero forward and backward consumption, so that sales orders decrement the forecast only within the same period.)

2. What is the purpose of using backward or forward consumption? It is beneficial to observe (and also to describe to planners) that same-period consumption—and consumption that is either backward or forward—accomplishes two different objectives:

- *Same-period Forecast Consumption:* This is intended to prevent double counting when calculating the total demand that will then be used to drive production, procurement or stock transfers. Same-period Forecast Consumption is one method of having forecasts and sales orders interoperate in a way that allows forecasts to serve as a placeholder for sales orders (forecasts are then gradually replaced by sales orders as time passes). However, forecast consumption is only one way to do this. There are at least two others, as I will explain in following section:

- *Forecast Consumption Outside of the Same Period:* This is designed to prevent over-ordering. Over-ordering can occur when consumption is limited to the same periods by disallowing backward or forward consumption. While sales orders that are higher than forecasts are considered in the total demand calculation, sales orders that are lower than the forecast are not considered in total demand. Therefore, a forward or backward consumption setting (*or both, as both backward and forward consumption can be configured in most supply planning systems*) allows sales orders in one period to search and consume forecasts that have not yet been consumed in other periods. Products that are ordered more frequently tend to be given shorter backward/forward consumption durations, while products that are ordered less frequently tend to be given longer durations.

Alternatives to Forecast Consumption

There are several alternatives to forecast consumption that can achieve similar ends.

1. *Take the Greater of the Forecast or the Sales Orders:* One alternative method is to simply take the larger of the two values. In this way there is no forecast consumption; the forecast equals total demand until the sales orders exceed the forecast, at which point the sales orders equal total demand. The relationship between sales orders and forecast can change along the time horizon. For instance, some companies take the larger of the forecast or sales orders until five days out from the current date. At that point the forecasts are removed from the supply planning system, the logic being that only the sales orders should count when close to the execution horizon.

2. *Within a Certain Horizon Do Not Count the Forecast:* This method is actually another timing setting in APO called the SNP Forecast Horizon: Horizon in calendar days, during which the forecast is not considered as part of the total demand. Within this horizon, SNP does not take the forecast into account when calculating total demand. Outside of this horizon, the system calculates total demand using either the forecast or sales orders (whichever value is larger), and the other demands (dependent demand, distribution demand, planned demand, and confirmed demand). For instance, if the SNP Forecast Horizon is set to three weeks, then within this first three weeks of the SNP Planning Horizon, only sales orders count as demand.

Consumption in GATP

While SNP has forecast consumption, GATP has allocation consumption. In addition, GATP has a little-used functionality called forecast checking.

1. *Allocation Consumption:* Allocation consumption in GATP is where the sales orders consume the allocations. For instance, let's say a customer has an allocation of 100 units for a product at a location. If an order comes in for fifty units, the forecast consumption is reduced by fifty units. When a subsequent order for the same product at the same location for seventy-five comes through a week later, it will only be fulfilled for fifty units, even if there is plenty of stock or planned stock at the location.

2. *GATP Forecast Checking:* GATP also has something called Check Against Forecast, about which SAP Help has this to say: *"You execute a check against the forecast if you want to know if enough planned independent requirements are available for the incoming sales orders."* When GATP is configured this way, the system essentially uses the forecast as the allocation. It is one way of configuring GATP, which in practice is not that commonly used.

Now that we have covered backward and forward consumption, we will move on to the next timing setting that can be set either forward or backward.

Backward and Forward Production Scheduling

Backward and forward production scheduling has more implications than backward and forward consumption. However, it is much simpler to understand because, while the primary goal of backward and forward consumption is to prevent over-ordering, backward and forward scheduling deals with "when" demand will be satisfied. Scheduling can be performed in two directions, but there are more than two options because the directions can be combined in one scheduling setting. Furthermore, different supply planning methods allow for different scheduling to be performed.

To understand how to use the different scheduling alternatives that are available in systems, it is important to begin with a definition of each of the scheduling types. SAP's definition of how the three scheduling options work in its system follows. These definitions apply for both SAP ERP and for SAP APO; however, other applications with supply and production planning functionality work very much the same.

1. *Forward Scheduling:* For the start date, the system uses the beginning of the period in which the production quantities were entered. From this start date, the system calculates in a forward direction to determine the finish date. The system displays the order quantities on the production start date.

2. *Backward Scheduling:* For the finish date, the system uses the end of the period in which the production quantities were entered. From this finish date, the system calculates in a backward direction to determine the start date.

3. *Backward/Forward Scheduling:* Here the system works in two steps:
   a. In the first step, the system uses the end of the period in which the production quantities were entered as the finish date. From this finish date, the system calculates in a backward direction to determine the start date.
   b. In the second step, the system uses the beginning of the period calculated in step one and then schedules forward. Order processing commences at the beginning of the start period calculated by the system and ends in the period specified by the planner.

Some systems such as MRP, which is the supply planning method in SAP ERP, are run with backward (then) forward scheduling by default. However, other supply planning methods, such as SAP CTM, do not have the ability to perform backward scheduling first and then forward scheduling, and can only perform either backward or forward scheduling in one planning run. Any supply planning system that is unconstrained must first perform backward scheduling. MRP is unconstrained and this is why there is no option to use only forward scheduling. SAP CTM has the ability to be constrained, and for this reason can be run with forward scheduling. In fact, with CTM, SAP does not offer the option to begin with backward scheduling and then move to forward scheduling, which is the default method of operation for MRP in SAP ERP.

More on backward and forward scheduling is available at that article below:

  http://www.scmfocus.com/sapplanning/2012/06/27/backward-scheduling-forward-scheduling-sap-erp-sap-apo/

Backward scheduling is the most common scheduling direction. Backward scheduling works from the need date, and calculates the activities necessary to provide material availability "backward" from the need date. Forward scheduling works much more simply, and schedules activities to take place as soon as possible, as if the material demand date is immediate. Performing forward scheduling only in a supply and initial production planning run (and no backward scheduling), "front loads" resources (also known as "fill to capacity"). When applied to internally produced items, machine and labor resources will be employed to product material prior to their need. One might observe that this is wasteful, but in fact the activity can be the correct action to take. Companies do not build capacity to match the peak demand periods throughout the year. Some companies will find themselves unable to meet capacity at certain times, meaning that they have the option of producing early, producing late (if the customer accepts late shipments), or denying the order. Furthermore, the setup involved in some products is significant when compared to the inventory carrying cost of keeping the material in stock. One company I worked with was able to produce a full year's demand for an item in three hours, but the setup time to produce this item was four hours. It would not make sense for them to break the single yearly production run into two ninety-minute runs to avoid storing inventory.

Understanding the Primary Benefit of Forward Scheduling

Forward scheduling (also known as front loading) with internal production is primarily a trade-off between producing early and carrying inventory, or not producing early, and not filling one's production capacity. Forward-scheduling allows a company to produce and procure before the system would ordinarily schedule (meaning more inventory is carried prior to the inventory being consumed). Because companies typically do not have unlimited factory capacity or material availability and also because some factories—repetitive manufacturing environments in particular—require long production runs in order to achieve their potential production efficiencies, the ability to forward-schedule production orders and their associated purchase orders can be the correct approach to configure a company's supply and production planning systems. More detail on forward scheduling is available at the link below:

http://www.scmfocus.com/sapplanning/2012/06/13/front-loading-resources-in-sap-snp/

The forward scheduling setting can be seen in the screen shot on the following page, which shows SAP CTM in the Planning Strategies sub-tab of the CTM Profile.

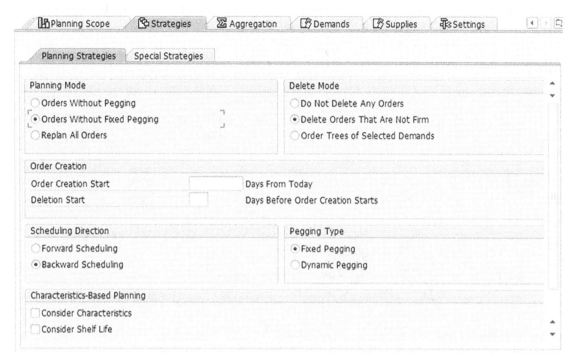

The options that are available with respect to backward and forward scheduling are very important for the output of the planning run. For instance, a procedure that begins with backward scheduling, and then switches to forward scheduling (which is the default for MRP in SAP ERP) will produce a very different output than one that begins with forward scheduling.

Scheduling Direction and Its Implications

As I have discussed, forward scheduling can be the correct setting in some circumstances. However, effectively leveraging APO to meet forward scheduling means more than simply changing the scheduling direction in the supply planning method. For instance, setting forward scheduling with CTM can lead to an interesting result, which is shown in the graphics on the following page. It can mean that higher priority customers, whose orders are run through the allocation supply planning procedure earlier, can consume a production resource sooner than they would ordinarily with backward scheduling. Forward scheduling plans all requirements as early as possible, without consideration for when the demand is actually needed, as is shown in the series of graphics on the following page:

Before the CTM Run

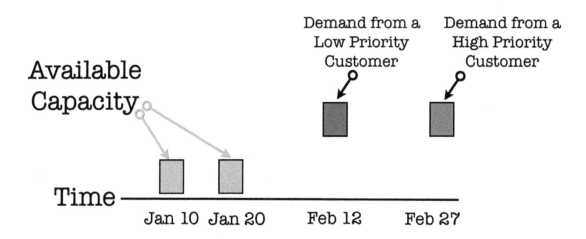

This is designed to show the state prior to the CTM run. Notice that there are two demands. The demand from the higher priority customer is farther out in the planning horizon than the demand from the lower priority customer.

The CTM Run with Backward Scheduling

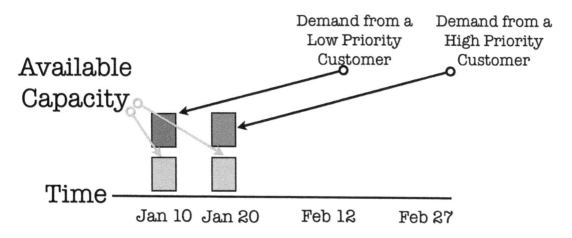

Under backward scheduling, as long as the demand from the higher priority customer can be met on time, the system will chose to peg or associate the demand with the later capacity.

The CTM Run with Forward Scheduling

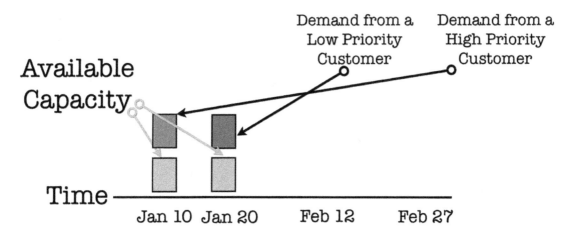

However, under forward scheduling, even if the demand from the higher priority customer can be met on time with the later capacity, CTM will assign the customer demand to the first available capacity. CTM does this because of the combination of CTM processing the higher priority customer prior to the low priority customer, along with the forward scheduling setting which plans all demands as soon as possible.

This is of course an undesirable outcome. However, there are several options, listed in the article below, to control this outcome and to prevent it from happening.

http://www.scmfocus.com/sapplanning/2012/08/08/effective-resource-front-loading-with-maximum-earliness-or-sequential-ctm-profiles/

Scheduling Direction When Using Cost Optimization

The supply planning method of cost optimization can also be made to perform forward scheduling. However, most often it will not have a setting for scheduling direction. Instead, the scheduling direction is controlled by the costs that are set up in the optimizer, notably the storage costs. Storage costs make the model incur a cost for each day that a product is kept at a location. The inclusion of storage costs therefore creates an incentive in the model to delay production until that product is required. Therefore, the use of a storage cost promotes backward scheduling. If storage costs are set to "0," many optimizers will immediately switch to forward scheduling. When storage costs are included, the optimizer switches to backward scheduling as it has now been provided with an incentive not to minimize inventory.

Backward and Forward Scheduling with Procurement and Stock Transfer Planning in SNP

Forward scheduling can be used to create planned production orders, purchase requisitions, or even stock transport requisitions prior to when they would be scheduled under backward scheduling. Companies routinely pull forward their procurement and stock transports in anticipation of future demand. Usually forward scheduling procurement and stock transfers are performed manually rather than set up in the supply chain planning systems. In order for forward scheduling to work in a way that meets the business requirements (and not simply initiate all activities immediately), it is necessary to constrain the resources over which the activities are spread.

In addition to demand spikes, there can be other reasons for forward scheduling. For instance, if suppliers are unreliable, then forward scheduling could reduce the risk of non-delivery or late delivery by creating purchase requisitions as soon as possible. Another reason for forward scheduling could be if the price of a material is predicted to rise in the future. Both situations can arise when an industry becomes capacity-constrained. Years ago this happened in the aerospace industry with titanium, with lead times becoming extended and so any part made of titanium was affected. In this situation, an alternative to forward scheduling is to adjust the lead times to make them represent the current environment.

As has been discussed throughout this book, it is common to plan with constrained production resources. It is much less common to plan with either supply planning resources (transportation resources, storage resources, etc.) or with the capacity constraints of suppliers (which would constrain the purchase requisitions).

The traditional output of a supply planning system is planned production orders, purchase requisitions and stock transfer requisitions Planned production orders and purchase requisitions are created by the initial/network supply planning run, and stock transfer requisitions are created by the deployment run. (I will cover forward scheduling in the deployment run shortly.) If the initial/network supply planning run is set to forward scheduling, it will forward-schedule planned production orders and purchase requisitions unless controlled in some way.

The scheduling direction for each supply planning recommendation type (production, procurement, transfer) should be analyzed and determined separately. That is, just because a company wants to front-load its production schedule does not necessarily mean it also wants to front-load or forward-schedule its purchase requisitions (for materials that are not part of a manufactured product) or its stock transfers. Therefore, the company must determine which recommendations from the supply plan they wish to forward-schedule and which they do not wish to forward-schedule, and then adjust the settings in the supply planning application accordingly. When it comes to the initial/network supply planning run, the decision of what to forward-schedule is quite important, because there are two types of recommendations (planning production orders and purchase requisitions) that come from this planning run, and the same scheduling direction may not work for both. Manufacturing companies may create purchase requisitions for products that are part of a manufacturing BOM, and also for products that are purchased and then resold. When forward scheduling is enabled and there are production capacity constraints, the purchase requisitions that are part of manufacturing BOMs will only be brought forward to the degree that there is manufacturing capacity. However, purchased materials that are not part of a manufacturing BOM will simply be brought forward as early as possible, unless the supplier's capacity is modeled and constrained. This is why it can make sense to place manufactured product along with the procured product that is an input to the manufactured product in one planning run and resold-procured product in a separate run.

Forward Scheduling and Capacity Leveling

Forward scheduling can be used with an unconstrained supply planning procedure, but the unconstrained network supply plan must be processed with a capacity-leveling procedure. The SNP capacity-leveling heuristic can be run with forward scheduling as is shown in the screen shot on the following page.

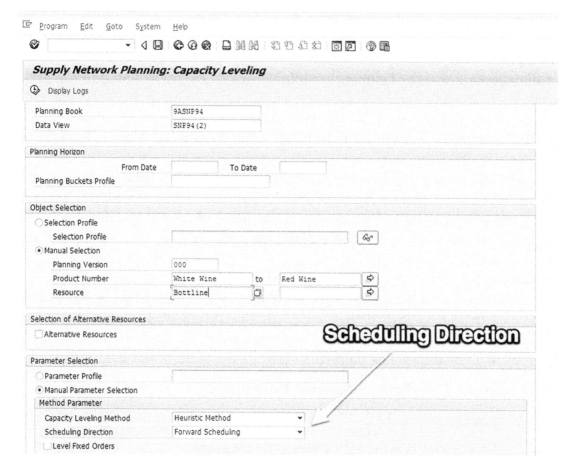

Capacity leveling is the second step when a non constraint-based method is used for supply or production planning. As can be seen from the screen shot above, in SNP, forward scheduling is an option, which I have selected.

Scheduling Direction and PP/DS

PP/DS has several forward-scheduling heuristics that can be used to essentially do the same thing as has been described with forward scheduling in SNP.

1. SAP_PMAN_002 – Infinite Forward Scheduling: Compact forward scheduling in the event of a scheduling delay in make-to-engineer or make-to-order production, based upon today's date or an entered date.

2. SAP_DS_01 – Stable Forward Scheduling: Used to resolve planning-related interruptions using several BOM levels (infinite).

A full explanation of the heuristics available in PP/DS can be found in the article below:

http://www.scmfocus.com/sapplanning/2008/09/21/ppds-and-snp-heuristics/

However, the issue with forward scheduling in PP/DS is that these heuristics can only forward-schedule for the PP/DS Planning Horizon, which is typically not longer than a month. This is why forward-scheduling requirements tend to fall onto SNP, as it has a far longer planning horizon.

Conclusion

This chapter covered a number of time-related settings that can be set to backward, forward, or backward then forward. The intent was to show the reader the similarities between these settings, even though they are distributed across different APO modules. The following settings were discussed in this chapter:

1. Backward and Forward Forecast Consumption

2. Consumption in GATP

3. Backward and Forward Production Scheduling

4. Backward and Forward Procurement and Stock Transfer Scheduling

We started with backward and forward forecast consumption as one way of dealing with the interaction between the forecast and sales orders. This technique prevents the natural over-ordering bias that occurs when consumption is used in a supply planning system. In periods where sales orders are less than the forecast, the forecast is taken as the total demand. Backward consumption consumed previous forecasts, while forward consumption consumes future forecasts. Most supply planning applications allow forward and backward consumption to be used at the same time, and the distance (or number of days that forecast consumption is in effect) can be configured, as shown in the screen shot on the following page for SAP SNP.

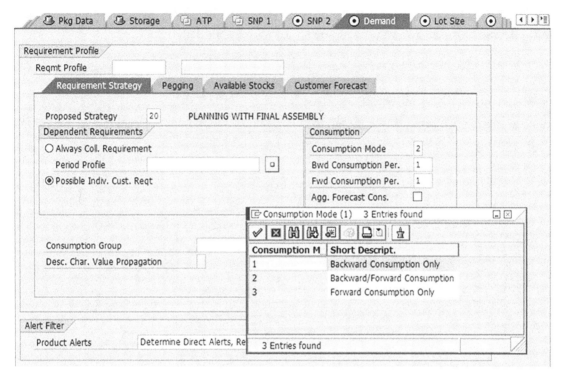

This screen shot shows how straightforward it is to add the scheduling direction and the length of forecast consumption. These settings are set in the Product Location Master in SNP and therefore are set at the product-location combination. This means that different combinations can have different forecast consumption settings.

Consumption and scheduling are important functionalities in supply planning systems. Because of their similar names, backward and forward consumption and backward and forward scheduling can sometimes be confused for one another.

Backward and forward scheduling is the implementation within the supply planning system of the company's policies with respect to how it will meet demand. The scheduling alternatives vary depending upon whether the supply plan (and initial production plan) is created in one step (that is capacity-constrained) or in a two-step (unconstrained) process, and these options also vary depending upon the system and the method that is used. For instance, in SAP ERP, MRP uses first backward then forward scheduling as the default scheduling method (also known as backward-forward scheduling). With the SNP capacity-leveling heuristic, forward or backward scheduling can be used. I show the SNP capacity-leveling heuristic screen below, which is set to forward scheduling.

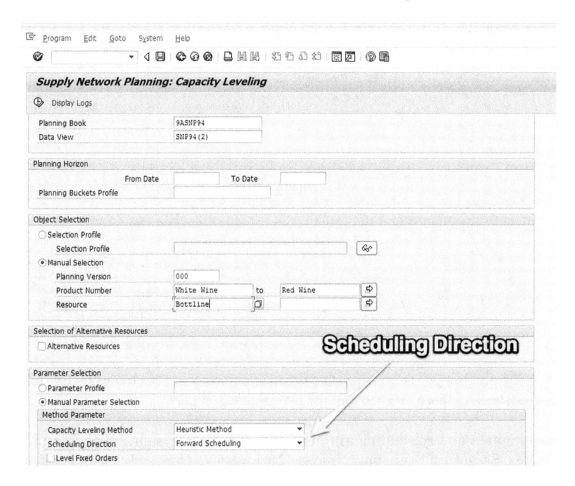

Capacity leveling is the second step in the two-step (that is, unconstrained) supply planning and initial production planning run. Cost optimization applications for supply planning generally control the scheduling direction with storage costs, and not with a defined setting that is more straightforward to understand. If storage costs are set to "0," there is no reason for the system not to move the planned production orders as forward as possible, while still meeting demand.

Forward scheduling, when used with the allocation/prioritization supply planning method, will often serve to further increase the status of high priority customers over low priority customers. When capacity is available earlier and later—both of which would satisfy the higher-priority customer demand under conditions of backward scheduling—with forward scheduling, the first demand that is processed will be allocated to the first available capacity slot. This action will tend to build more inventory earlier, in some cases quite a bit earlier than it needs to be. However, adjustments can be made to control this outcome. The scheduling direction setting is very important and the same system with all the same configuration systems—except for different scheduling directions—will provide very different results.

One reason for using forward scheduling for manufactured items is to meet the needs of repetitive manufacturing, which must run in a relatively constant manner in order to attain potential production output and efficiencies. Other reasons for using forward scheduling include the need to pre-produce in order to meet spikes in demand or to batch the production for items with short production runs in relation to their set-up times.

Companies will often want to make scheduling direction decisions for their manufactured products and their procured products independently of each other, and if the decision is made to use a different scheduling direction for each, then the supply planning system can, in many cases, be set to incorporate different products into different profiles that are identical except for the products included in the profile and the scheduling direction. This is entirely controllable within the settings and the master data selections of many supply planning applications.

Not all products need to follow the same scheduling direction, and not all products need to be scheduled the same way through all times in the year.

CHAPTER 6

Capacity Planning with S&OP and the MPS

S&OP is a relatively recent term first coined in the 1980's. However, corporations large and small have used the process for decades. And if we think about it, it is quite logical to believe that as long as people have coordinated with each other to accomplish goals, we have held S&OP meetings.

Take the building of the pyramids, for example:

1. Someone had to **forecast** how many cut slabs of stone could be placed upon the pyramid (the demand).

2. This forecast had to be used to **plan** how many people would be cutting the slabs, and capacity of the barge that carried the slab up the Nile (the supply).

3. The person financing the operation needed to determine how much funding they had to allow for this many workers, this many barges, etc. (the financial plan).

This is the heart of the S&OP process. The ancient Egyptians may have been performing the calculations on scrolls rather than software, but S&OP is a process **independent of a technology**. Until recently S&OP has been primarily facilitated with spreadsheets, and more recently specialized applications have supported the process. With constant technological developments, who knows what will be used in the future? So while S&OP is a recently derived term, the process it describes is a few millennia old.

If we go back in time a bit, we used a different term to describe a slightly different process -- master production schedule or MPS. The term MPS was used interchangeably with the term MRP, but this is incorrect. MPS items are run separately from either the normal MRP run (if one is using SAP ERP exclusively for planning). Critical product materials are typically placed in the MPS category, while non-critical materials are placed in the MRP category.

An MPS run combines three restrictions that relate to the **product dimension, timing and the bill of materials.**

1. *Using Subset of the Overall Database*: The reason for making the MPS run a subset of the overall product database is two-fold. First. the MPS run is **only for critical** materials. (Criticality could be based upon profitability of the item, importance within a product line, materials that have raw materials, components or subcomponents that are limited in some way, or any number of other reasons defined by the company.) A second reason, which is now dated, is that earlier computer systems were limited in processing capabilities. In order to get the MPS to run in a timely manner, and possibly to run it multiple times, it was important to limit the amount of data the system had to process.

2. *The Timing and Planning Horizon*: The MPS must already be performed prior to the network or initial planning thread. This is not a statement regarding the specific sequence of the run in the schedule, but rather what the **MPS has evaluated versus when the same time frame is "analyzed" by the MPS run**. Obviously, a simulation run like the MPS would make little sense if it were run after or at the same time as the initial planning run.

3. *Limiting the BOM Explosion:* In other words, the raw materials, components, sub-components are not all multiplied (or "exploded") by the

demand for the finished goods. Instead, the BOM may only be exploded a limited number of levels down from the finished good. This is a less detailed type of analysis that is more focused on some areas rather than others (such as manufacturing rather than material constraints). However, with the improvements in computer hardware, the reduction in the degree of BOM explosion is another feature, which is increasingly dated.

The MPS does a number of things. Some of these are shorter term in nature and focused on capacity leveling, and others are **longer term in nature and focused on capacity planning**. However, MPS is becoming less used as a process and as a term in the industry. In fact, S&OP is replacing the parts of the MPS process that are **capacity planning in nature**. It is currently very common to hear the term S&OP within companies and increasingly rare to hear the term MPS.

Interestingly, the growth in S&OP has not lead to a corresponding increase in the use of S&OP applications. The vast majority of S&OP "systems" are worked out in spreadsheets and, interestingly, most of the S&OP applications either look like spreadsheets or have areas that allow porting out to a spreadsheet.

S&OP systems have, for the most part, relied upon output from other applications: supply planning, demand planning, and production planning systems, for example. Data from these other tools are often imported and then converted to a financial analysis to be fed to an S&OP system. Some vendors have now introduced functionality where the **planning processing** is performed in the S&OP system rather than in the systems that traditionally fed S&OP systems with output. Because of this, a number of complex issues arise regarding reconciliation, which are covered in depth in the SCM Focus Press book *Sales & Operations Planning in Software*.

Capacity Leveling, S&OP, and Aggregation

S&OP is an aggregated planning process. Therefore, one of the major questions which arises during S&OP planning is how to manage the planning hierarchy.

"One of the hottest discussion points during the (re)design of an

S&OP process is the level of detail. While some people strive to the highest possible detail, others push to look only at global figures. Both parties have a point. The "detailists" often argue that it is impossible to check the impact of certain constraints, such as production constraints or customer requirements on a global level. As a result, they aim for a plan on customer-article level.

The "globalists" position themselves on the other side of the spectrum, arguing that S&OP should only look at the big lines. They conclude that S&OP should operate on 4 or 5 big product families."

– Sales and Operations Planning, How to
Avoid the 5 Key Pitfalls

Globalists argue that S&OP should be restricted in product scope (much like the MPS described previously). They also argue that the S&OP process should be performed not on products, but on "product families" that are aggregations along product dimensions.

The Pros and Cons of Detailed Planning

Executives are most comfortable with an aggregated level of planning, and S&OP is an **executive planning process**. However, actual feasibility can't be determined if the process is kept only at an aggregated level. For example, if during planning at the product family level, and product family components are made using different resources without first knowing the demand for each, there is inadequate detail to conduct sufficient supply planning. This results in the uncomfortable situation of pitting the expertise of the participants in the S&OP process against that of those in the supply chain planning process.

Unconstrained Planning

S&OP is normally run in an unconstrained manner and, therefore, performed in an adjustable way. This allows observation and analysis of the full difference between demand and supply. However, rather than attempting to move demand, analysis determines whether it's worthwhile to adjust capacity. The options here can be quite numerous. An example could include simply buying new machinery, or retrofitting an existing but underutilized production line, or building a new factory. These are just a few examples emphasizing the variety of options often available. And, of course, other areas outside of manufacturing are also open to investment – adding more trucks, adding employees, etc.

System Overlap and Planning Domain Expertise

Two major issues affect the aggregation level in an effective S&OP model. The first is the overlap between supply and demand planning and the S&OP application. The second is the question of who handles S&OP and whether they have domain expertise to independently perform detailed planning.

1. *The Question of Planning Overlap*: S&OP software should not attempt to give the impression that it is replicating the planning that occurs in supply chain planning applications. For instance, production-planning systems have incorporated setup data into the planning run. The setup information is designed to allow for feasible and optimal production sequences, say, moving the production sequence from lighter paints to darker paints before scheduling a cleanup that will result in the shortest possible downtime. Without this setup data, a system will assume there is no downtime between manufacturing changeovers, which a) is untrue, and b) will result not only in an incorrect or unrealistic production sequence, but is **also in dangerous overestimates of true capacity**. If the S&OP system accepts the supply and production plan from the supply chain planning system, then it leverages this detail. Most seasoned analysts would tell you that the preferred approach is sacrificing some ability to adjust the S&OP model in exchange for more realistic projections produced by trained professionals with access to details not generally possessed by executives.

2. *The Question of Domain Expertise*: To make usable adjustments, the person planning must have **domain expertise with the products and factors related to the products.** Planning and adjustments without the necessary domain expertise eliminates the value of performing the planning process.

Interpretation and Planning of Consensus Planning Processes

While S&OP is a consensus planning process, a great deal of research goes into it. The real story about the consensus planning processes is considerably more complicated than is normally presented, and the results are far less encouraging in that good outcomes can be obtained without considerable design effort placed into the process. In fact, consensus-planning processes are very much a process of receiving input and then **performing analytical filtering to remove or reduce the impact of individuals or groups with poor forecasting or other input accuracy**. This part of consensus planning processes is under emphasized, probably because it's not as appealing as the story of simply increasing participation. The next logical question is, *"Who is going to get their input reduced?"*, which then begs the question of how to raise this topic during the implementation of consensus planning processes.

Research into Consensus-Based Forecasting by RAND

What we now consider consensus-based forecasting was first formally studied at the RAND Institute, which then developed the Delphi Method. Named after the ancient Greek city whose Oracles were consulted by Greeks and Romans, the Delphi Method is now just one method of performing consensus-based forecasting.

RAND's research into the Delphi Method began in 1943 when they performed numerous studies on it, intending to obtain better group judgment. For example, they researched how the effect of strong personality types on groups can be mitigated. Since then, consensus-based planning methods have been studied in a number ways and applied to a wide variety of disciplines. The majority of academic research in consensus-based forecasting is outside of supply chain management and is concentrated in areas such as finance and, specifically, trading. However, it's important to know that S&OP is **not** the Delphi Method and, in fact, as usually performed, S&OP meetings face all of the same pitfalls as often found in research of consensus-based forecasting.

The Delphi Method is a remote approach with structured rules to control for too much influence coming from any one participant. Combined with the common feature within companies for certain branches to have more political power than others, it means that S&OP, as often practiced, is **quite susceptible to overwhelming influence coming from the stronger participants**. This observation goes virtually unmentioned in the general literature on S&OP. That is, even though the evidence is clear that consensus -based methods where each individual's input is publicly known, this leads to some individuals exercising disproportionate influence on the overall output.

CHAPTER 7

The Relationship Between Planning Systems and S&OP Systems

How planning systems and S&OP interact is an important question because it is not well covered in S&OP publications. As I pointed out in the introduction, none of the books written up to the point of this book's publication have focused on the available S&OP systems, and most articles have little from the systems perspective. Instead, publications on S&OP have tended to be written from the perspective of strategies and theory. In fact, the vast majority of consulting in S&OP tends to be from the strategy side. Therefore, the systems' details are going to tend to be overlooked. Once one delves into the details of using S&OP applications, alongside external planning systems, many issues that must be resolved become apparent. We will begin this chapter by describing the normal relationship between planning systems and S&OP systems, before describing how new S&OP applications like SAP IBP and Anaplan have changed that traditional relationship.

Services S&OP

This book focuses on S&OP for companies with a supply chain, either manufacturers or distributors, since this is where most of the S&OP-related focus lies. One of the interesting aspects of writing this book was searching for material on S&OP in the services sector and seeing how little there was to read. However, S&OP is a universal process, as every entity must balance supply and demand. For whatever reason, S&OP receives light coverage with respect to service industries.

If we consider a bank, it's clear that the same issues of balancing supply and demand that would apply to a manufacturing company, also apply to S&OP. In fact, given how phone support customer service quality has declined over the past several decades, and how wait times have dramatically increased, (one of the favorite messages which plays on support lines is *we are facing abnormally high call volumes, thank your for your patience*"). In addition to outsourcing phone support to very low cost countries that have lower quality English skills, one might ask how good a job service companies are doing with respect to their S&OP processes as they have clearly cut quality, costs and capacity – but have generally not reduced the prices for insurance, banking, etc. These are some of the most elementary types of planning and yet they are beyond so many companies that can't see past cutting costs and fail to realize that they may be hurting their sales. The relationship between investment and sales and profit is what S&OP is all about. Here, we see how disconnected executives have become from the central issue in S&OP

> *"In fact 90% of executives see Customer Service as crucial to their future business success. In the same study more than 70% of senior call center executives revealed that their companies fail to meet their customers' expectations, according to Bain. So we have a strange dichotomy. Organizations know that good customer service is essential to their future success; they understand that there is a real tangible cost and risk of dissatisfied customers defecting and yet these same organizations seem incapable of affecting change."*
> — Why is Most Call Center Service so Bad?

This performance is mirrored in the customer's perception. According to Lee

Resources, while 80% of companies think they deliver superior service, only 8% of their customers think the same thing.

This brings up the topic of how companies understand the value produced by their call centers.

> *"In fact, for many organizations it is the primary communications channel and the only meaningful one that facilitates a two way discussion, a dialogue. Failing to recognize this fact leads organizations to undervalue the contribution the call center and broader customer service and technical support plays in sustaining the business. Not only can a call center generate revenue through orders, up-sell and extensions, but the call center also protects revenue already promised through solving issues and fixing problems, many of which were not caused or created by the call center."*
>
> – Why is Most Call Center Service so Bad?

This is a misunderstanding of how service affects the company's bottom line. Companies that score the worst in call center customer service, companies like Citibank, American Airlines, Comcast, Blue Cross Blue Shield, Bank of America, etc have big advertising budgets, but don't put the money they need to into call centers. Are these companies that understand the relationship between investing in their service capacity and their bottom line?

A certain number of customers will call on the phone to a call center or walk through any bank door, or ask for a number of services with which the employees must be fully versed, and the bank must balance demand and supply. Therefore, they must, in some way, perform a high-level match between supply and demand, and find a way to fund this – that is, they must engage in some form of S&OP process. Booz Allen Hamilton wrote a paper that covers S&OP specifically in the financial services industry and brought up the following questions faced by financial services companies.

- "How much call waiting time should be allowed for different customer segments?

- How long should the queues in our branches be allowed to grow?

- How short should our account processing lead-time be?

- How long should it take for our new customers to open an account, or buy a policy from us?

- How accurate should our response rates be?

- How should we prioritize new product introductions?

- What type of flexibility should we build into our operational capacity, taking into account the cost/service trade off?"

Therefore, I wanted to establish that services S&OP is just as important as S&OP for manufacturers and distributors.

For purely service companies, S&OP applications must be integrated with different types of software that are specific to their needs, a good example of this being call center software. Software like TalkDesk or ZenDesk, records the timing and duration of calls, and create a database that can be used as the basis for further analyses. This create a usage history, which can then be correlated with the sales forecast to predict how many more resources will be required to service different types of calls. Overall, the question of adding supply is much simpler than in manufacturing, as the capacity normally comes down to adding or subtracting people or adjusting the systems that these people use. I will now continue discussing the implication of supply chain planning systems with S&OP, fully cognizant that services S&OP would not use a supply chain planning system.

The Traditional Interaction between S&OP and Planning Systems

Traditionally, the S&OP system is fed by the output of supply chain planning systems combined with financial data, which includes the price and the cost of the item. For the vast majority of companies, at the time of this book's publishing, they still perform S&OP without the use of an application, and instead with spreadsheets. Unless they put a high degree of effort into creating a very detailed S&OP spreadsheet and updating it with information regarding constraints, the company will **not** have the ability to do much more than incorporate the final forecast with the final supply plan and to dollarize the resulting inventory position. Therefore the following are often what is sent to S&OP systems from either an external planning system or the ERP system.

1. The Forecast

2. The Supply Plan

3. Costs and Prices

Costs and prices allow the dollarization of the sales and operations plan, and costs allow for things like inventory costs to be calculated, while the inclusion of prices allows profitability to be calculated.

We can look at an application that represents this type of S&OP, although it is both a demand and supply planning system as well as an S&OP system. This application is called Demand Works Smoothie.

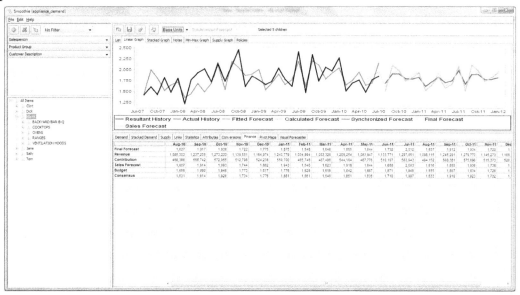

In Demand Works Smoothie, one can see the dollarization of the forecast.

Forecast adjustment is used to perform simulation. If demand increased by different amounts what would be the effect on the system? This forecast adjustment should not be confused with the actual forecast, which has been determined through extensive demand planning and sales forecasting.

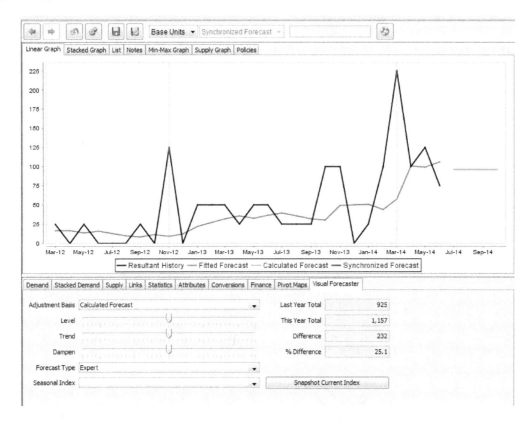

Demand Works Smoothie has one of the easiest ways to adjust the forecast.It employs sliders. Here we begin with the sliders in a neutral state.

S&OP is performed at a high level of aggregation. Therefore, when a change is made it is necessary that the change be applied to a grouping, rather than having to make the change to each product location combination at a time – which would be impossible in an S&OP setting. In fact any application that is used for S&OP must be very effective at grouping products and geographies.

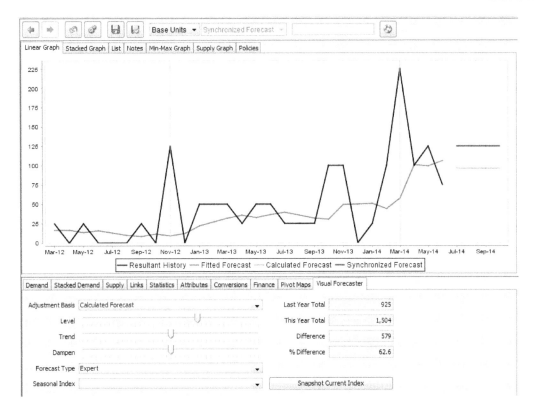

*This shows the **level** of the forecast brought up. So the forecast is now higher by the percentage that I moved the slider. This adjustment using the sliders can be performed at any level of the hierarchy, from a single SKU to all of the products and all of the locations in one fell swoop. After the forecast has been adjusted, Smoothie can run the supply plan.*

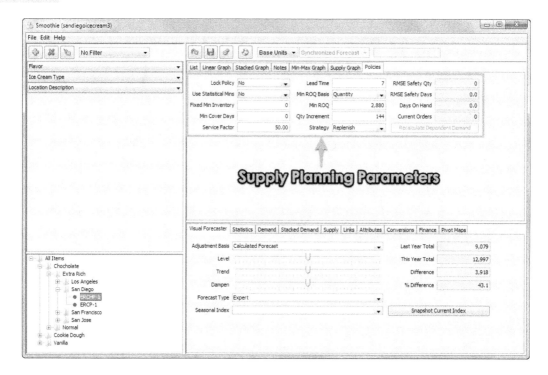

The same aggregation functionality that was shown in the previous forecast adjustment screen shot is also useful for supply planning. These are the supply planning parameters. They control the supply plan, and they can be changed for any grouping that is selected. For instance a minimum number of coverage days (which controls inventory level) could be set for either the entire product database or for only parts of the product database. A company could simulate the changes brought about by paying more to suppliers which would allow the specific component's lead time to decline, decreasing the lead time for the overall finished good. This could be done by selecting only the components for which the program is applicable and changing the lead-time for all of them, and then recalculating the supply plan.

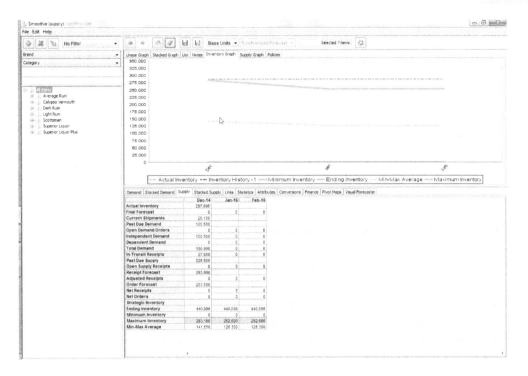

This view shows the supply plan. The supply plan can be run very easily off of the menu.

Because S&OP is integrated into Smoothie, any change made to the demand plan and supply plan is **immediately shown** in the S&OP tab of the application, greatly reducing the complexity of integrating a separate S&OP system to the demand and supply planning system. This is an important distinction that it can be difficult to get across to executive decision makers during a demo. One caveat is that Smoothie does not deal with production beyond the application of the production lot size that can be added to Smoothie's master data parameters. Smoothie is not a production planning system, and therefore Smoothie does not deal with manufacturing resources. This means, as with other systems which are similarly designed, that there is no restriction or even any visibility to the scheduling of overcapacity.

What we've just shown is the most common approach to S&OP in systems in terms of what is modeled, except that, in Smoothie, demand, supply and S&OP planning are all done from within one application. When the demand and supply planning systems and S&OP are all separate from one another, this requires integration, increases the time lag, and reduces the ability of the S&OP application to be rerun without becoming out of synch with the demand and supply planning systems.

This approach is not comprehensive, however, it provides a system with a reasonable overhead. It also prevents the executives from making many adjustments to the demand, supply or production plan. I will explain further on why this is a good thing. Now we will move on to the more advanced S&OP applications.

The More Advanced Approach to S&OP

Please note, I didn't title this subsection "a better approach" since it is far from clear that advanced approaches produce better results in the real world. That being said, the more advanced approach has the S&OP application incorporating some of the master data from existing planning systems and producing its own plans, rather than merely parroting back the preliminary supply and demand plans done in isolation. Under this design, the following information is sent to the S&OP system. The bold items are new or net change from the previous list.

1. The Forecast

2. **Sales history**

3. Costs and Prices

4. The Supply Plan

5. **Capacities** (sent from the supply planning/production planning system, includes things like resource capacity, downtime, resource availability times per day, etc..)

6. **Lot Sizing** (sent from the supply planning/production planning system.)

7. **Reorder Points** (sent from the supply planning/production planning system.)

SAP IBP includes the ability of SAP to generate a **statistical forecast** (as opposed to simply receiving a forecast from the external forecasting system).

It also has the ability to **run heuristics** that produce a supply and production plan, rather than simply representing the supply/production plan from elsewhere.

A Standard S&OP Process

If we look at a standard S&OP process, it looks something like the following:

1. *Review and Sign Off on the Demand Plan:* It all begins with demand. Therefore, in order to progress through the S&OP process, this first step must be accomplished.

2. *Review and Sign Off on the Supply Plan*: The supply plan contains both the inventory that will need to be brought into the supply network and the production that is to be performed by the company (in the case where the company in question is a manufacturer).

3. *Review and Sign Off on the Financial Plan*: The financial plan is dependent upon the finalization of the supply plan.

Review and Sign Off on the Demand Plan

It should first be pointed out that, in terms of **normal supply chain planning**, not all companies actually **need** to forecast demand for their products in order to run their business. For example, defense contractors frequently know years in advance what they will be building because they have firm government contracts that contain quantities and dates. This is called a **build to order** or **make to order** manufacturing environment.[1]

Defense contractors receive their sales orders so far out that the sales order simply takes the place of a forecast. And the sales orders are further out than the combined lead-time for both procurement and manufacturing. This greatly improves the ability to plan as the supply plan can be based on a known

---

[1] An important feature of the various manufacturing environments is that the **relationship** between the demand signal and the beginning of production orprocurement is not always the same for all of the products in the BOM or recipe.Manufacturing environments are covered in the SCM Focus Press book, *Replenishment Triggers: Setting Systems for Make to Stock, Make to Order & Assemble to Order*.

quantity rather than a forecast, which will always have some degree of error. The S&OP process for a build to order company is, as such, much simpler. It means that the sales plan (rather than the demand plan) is confirmed quickly, and the company can move quickly into supply plan confirmation. The manufacturing environments that are available to a company have less to do with what the company "wants to do," and more to do with the particular product the company produces combined with the type of market into which the product is sold. So while most companies would, if they had the option, prefer to be "make to order" environments to reduce supply chain complexity and costs, in reality, most companies must follow the make to stock manufacturing strategy because their procurement and manufacturing lead times are longer than the customer is willing to wait. However, in terms of S&OP, **all companies, make to order, assemble to order and make to stock alike** need to develop a financial forecast – not for supply chain planning but to **determine how to setup and constrain the business**. Make to order businesses may (if the sales orders are far enough out) use the sales orders as the "forecasts" for the S&OP process. However, most companies are not make to order, and therefore most companies do need to produce a **supply chain forecast**. This means that a forecast will almost always precede the forecast that is produced/adjusted in the S&OP process.

How Many Forecasts?

Within companies often the term "the forecast" is used. As in "the forecast is not accurate." However, any company conducting a proper planning strategy will have multiple forecasts. There is a sales forecast, a supply chain forecast, a marketing forecast, and so on. All of these must be coalesced into a single forecast for S&OP. The final forecast exists outside of the S&OP system. That is to say, a final forecast must be generated **whether or not an S&OP process exists**.

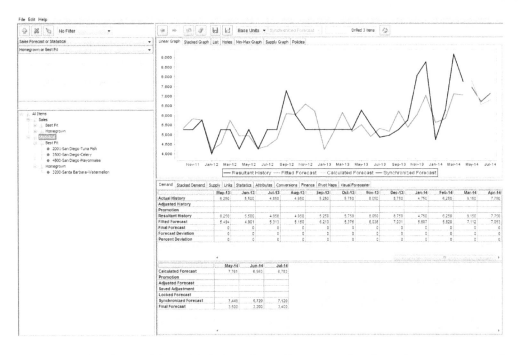

In Demand Works Smoothie, which is primarily a supply planning system, notice the row titled "Final Forecast" in the screen shot above. Most demand planning systems have a row, which represents the final forecast.

Review and Sign off on the Supply Plan

After the demand plan is agreed to, the supply plan review and sign off can begin. A supply plan (which contains, within it, the production plan), in a make to stock and assemble to order environment – where a forecast is produced either at the finished good or at the assembly level – means triggering supply. Replenishment triggers are actions that cause replenishment to occur. The term replenishment is easy to comingle in one's mind with purchasing. However, the replenishment strategy drives both procured materials and produced materials. To replenish simply means **to fill again**. But when we speak about replenishment, we're not just discussing the inventory to be sold, we're also talking about the raw materials needed to produce the inventory and support its manufacturing.A replenishment trigger can be either demand-based (from a forecast or a sales order falling into a particular planning bucket) or supply-based, in the form of a reorder point (a level of stock or raw material at which point a re-supply order is triggered).

Supply and production planning systems can be capacity constrained. Constraint-based planning works by setting up resources, anything from factory equipment to transportation units to handling equipment, in the model. Resources are then assigned limitations in capacity and/or availability (e.g., they have a specific capacity and can only be run from 8 a.m. to 10 p.m.).

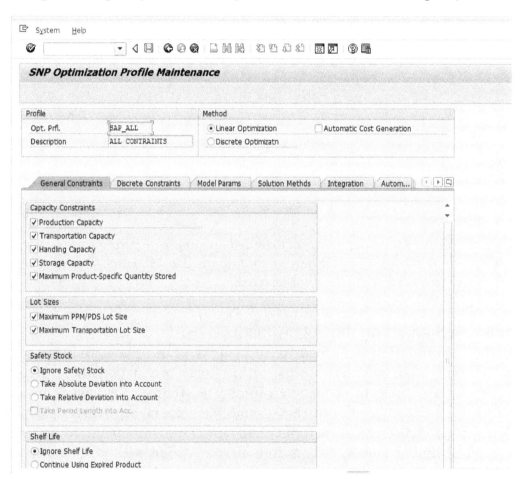

*In SAP APO, the supply-planning module, called SNP, can constrain on different types of resources. A constraint is something that restricts the capacity of the system. Supply and production planning systems that can constrain, allow resources to be constrained or unconstrained, that is not all resources that are setup in a these systems is necessarily constrained. All of this allows the application to create a "feasible plan" which means that the application will **not attempt to meet demand in a way that exceeds the capacity of the system.***

Constraining is the more sophisticated way of producing a supply and production plan. The other way is to perform capacity leveling.[2] Constraining a resources also allows for more effective multi-level planning, and constraint based planning means less manual work in capacity leveling, but it also requires a more sophisticated set of a capabilities in the implementing company and more investment into setting up the system.

Capacity Leveling

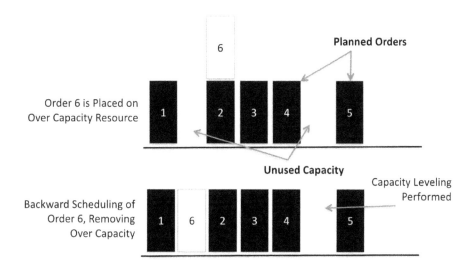

In capacity leveling, the leveling is performed either by a procedure or manually. The top portion of the graphic is after the initial or network supply planning run. This

---

[2] With unconstrained planning (or infinite planning), capacities may or may not be declared—and, if they are declared, there is nothing to stop the system from placing an unlimited load on any resource. A second planning pass called the capacity-leveling run must then adjust this. This topic is referred to as capacity planning. The details behind the differences between constraint based planning and capacity leveling are very important, particularly with respect to how capacity is managed at various levels of the bill of material. If you'd like to learn more about constraints on supply chain planning, we recommend you follow up with the SCM Focus Press book: *Constrained Supply and Production Planning in SAP APO*.

All of this has important implications for performing capacity planning in the S&OP system as systems like SAP IBP, that is S&OP systems that perform capacity management within the application.

*places the demand upon the resource based upon the need date, which is in turn based upon the need date (minus the lead times). When capacity is not constrained, there is no consideration given to what is feasible. Then, the capacity leveling process moves the planned production order from periods, which are **over capacity** to periods, which have **capacity**. The lower portion of the graphic above is after capacity leveling has been performed.*

In some S&OP systems, the resource data, as with the example provided previously with Demand Works Smoothie, is not copied over from either the ERP system or the external planning system. Not all companies employ **external supply chain planning systems** and those that don't tend to rely very heavily on spreadsheets as planning within ERP systems which is normally quite limiting.

Resources get a huge amount of attention in supply and production planning; however, the resource is only one of the types of constraints that are modeled by a supply chain planning system. Therefore, if the plan is not simply sent from the supply chain planning system to the S&OP system, it would need to similarly be **modeled** in the S&OP system. Another constraint is the production order batch or lot sizes. This is the minimum quantity in which a material is either procured or produced. Production lot sizes simply declare the batch in which an order must be produced (500 units, 1000 units, etc.) without declaring whether or not that lot size quantity is feasible, or if there is any capacity to produce that item requested by the supply planning system. For example, a production order may be created for 500 units on a specific day, but in actual fact, the resource is not available to produce 500 units on that day because it is out for maintenance. Another example of a constraint is the factory calendar, which determines **when** the factory can accept capacity.

The traditional output of a supply planning system is planned production orders— purchase requisitions and stock transfer requisitions. Planned production orders and purchase requisitions are created by the initial/network supply planning run, and stock transfer requisitions are created by the deployment run.

Deployment Plan

After the initial or network supply plan is generated, a second process, referred to as the deployment plan, is necessary. While the initial or network supply plan brings material into the supply network and schedules production orders, the **deployment plan moves the material through the supply network and out to customers**. This deployment plan is generated within the supply planning application.

Now that we have discussed finalizing the demand and supply plan, we can move to the financial plan.

Review and Sign off on the Financial Plan

The financial plan is a dependent entity based upon the supply (and production) plan. For manufacturing and distribution companies, the first obvious financial implication is inventory. When a specific average inventory position is calculated, it means a **specific allocation of capital in order to fund that inventory level.** The normal overhead costs are included which includes the office overhead, along with factory overhead, etc. Overhead of existing expenditures is already known by finance before arriving at an S&OP meeting, so finance is looking for the costs of things that are dependent upon the supply plan. Finance will have funded the company up to the present point, and therefore is looking for net change costs. The S&OP planning process is one of the few planning processes within a company where the constraints can be questioned and changed. Therefore, while other planning processes are about working within the existing constraints, S&OP is very much about **challenging the existing constraints**. If we can take a specific example, when there is too much demand for a particular period, supply chain planning tries to backwards or forward schedule the demand on the existing resource. However, in S&OP, if the plan shows long-term overcapacity, the S&OP process is to determine if it makes financial sense to add capacity. And in fact, this brings up an important point -- that it is unlikely that the executives will be able to redo the work of managing demand within the existing constraints better than the planners -- the primary value of the S&OP process is in changing the existing constraints or in evaluating if the existing constraints are worth changing.

Global Versus Regional S&OP

Although not frequently discussed as one would think, a big part of S&OP is at what geographic level it is performed. Various S&OP processes at different hierarchies in geography can mean including the S&OP process below it. This also means that there are **multiple** S&OP meetings throughout the month, and that the higher S&OP meetings are dependent upon the meeting outcomes below them. In fact, for larger companies in particular, it can be quite a bit of work just scheduling all of the meeting and managing the flow of plans from the regional up to the national then global S&OP processes. Each meeting has an assigned group of individuals. Some companies create a matrix, which lays out which individuals are assigned to which groups. Ultimately, one person should own each of the meetings, which is the same person that has the ultimate final approval for the S&OP plan for that particular area. One of the issues with S&OP that reduces its buy-in is that many S&OP meetings end up being rehashes of information that was discussed in other forums, and the moderator is unwilling to enforce the meeting topic to be constrained to the S&OP topics specifically.

	Country Plan			Global Plan	
1.	Country Plan Summary	View product level country plan vs. global target	6.	Global Target Summary	- View yearly sales and profit targets - Compare growth % by country
2.	Price Input	- Configure sales price increase at category and brand level - View YoY sales price growth	7.	Sales Target Set	- Define yearly global sales targets
3.	Volume Input	- Set volume growth on market assumptions - Run market growth and share scenarios	8.	Net Sales Summary	- Analyze yearly sales growth by geo - Compare product yearly sales targets
4.	Brand Positioning Summary	- Examine product's position within the market	9.	Target Allocation by Brand & Innovation	- Define target allocation by brand - Measure incremental sales from new product innovation
5.	Advertising & Promotion Input	- Create A&P cost assumptions based on market position	10.	Target Allocation by Country	- View target allocation by geo based on historical YoY growth
			11.	Profit Margin Target Set	- Define yearly PBO margin targets

Here we can see Anaplan allows the individual to go right into the area that is applicable. After changes have been made at the regional level, they roll up to the levels above this automatically.

Timing When to Expand Capacity

Within the discussion of capacity planning and adding capacity with capital improvements, the question of timing is always important. The company does not want to add capacity too soon – and risk not being able to use the capacity, or having to repurpose the capacity, and does not want to add capacity too late, as it will miss out on market opportunities and therefore profits. If we think outside of manufacturing and distribution for a moment, real estate is a perfect example of this conundrum. Economic cycles are difficult to predict, but building must be planned years in advance of the anticipated opening date. Many large-scale hotels were greenlit to be built right before the great recession of 2007-2008. The recession hit as several hotels were being built, and they suffered from low occupancy for years as Las Vegas tourist volumes too quite some time to recover. Clearly, many of those hotels would have never been built if the backers had a crystal ball.

> *"The timing variable in a capacity strategy is concerned with the balance between the forecasted demand for capacity and the supply of capacity. If there is a capacity demand surplus the utilization will be high, thus enabling a low cost profile, but there is also a risk of losing customers due to long delivery lead times. A capacity supply surplus on the other hand creates a higher cost profile by due to surplus capacity it is easier to maintain high delivery reliability and flexibility. The capacity strategy can thus be expressed as a tradeoff between high utilization and maintaining a capacity cushion."*
> – Linking the Perspectives from Manufacturing Strategy and
> Sales Operations Planning

A company can choose when to expand capacity and can be aggressive or less aggressive. This tradeoff is shown in the following graphic.

Adding Resource Capacity

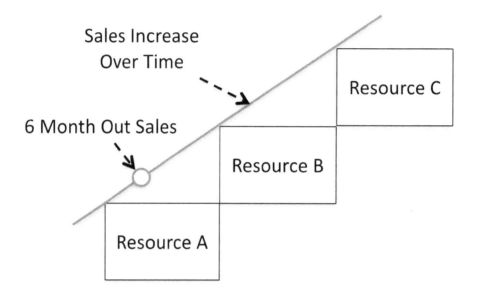

Resources ordinarily must be added as discrete units, while demand increases tend to be continuous. A pattern may be determined, and forecasted that eventually will require adding a resources in order to satisfy demand. However, when exactly these resources should be added can be up for debate. It can be possible to run the existing re-source or resource overtime by adding labor and extending the factory operating hours. This can allow for the postponement of the purchase and installation of the resource until later when the demand has grown even more and the utilization of the resource is more or less guaranteed. Certainly the cost of the resource will play into this decision, as will the profitability of the product, which is produced on the resource.

Conclusion

Everyone seems to love talking about the opportunity of S&OP. However, the details of how to connect S&OP systems to the systems that supply them with information are not yet fully realized in current software. There are a number of important decisions to be made that influence how the S&OP process will be managed and what level of planning will be performed, as well as how much the existing planning results will be accepted versus being modified by the executives in the S&OP meeting. Secondly, modification on the part of executives will mean having to incorporate those changes back to the various lower-level plans.

This chapter was careful to point out that while S&OP literature, including this book admittedly tends to very strongly focus on S&OP for manufacturers and distributors. However, S&OP is just as much needed in service industries as the need to balance long-term supply and demand, and to perform long-term budgeting and capital improvement planning is universal. Two common questions for service companies are:

- How long should queues be allowed to grow?
- How long should processes like the opening of a new account be allowed to take?

The traditional approach to S&OP for manufacturers and distributors is to feed S&OP spreadsheets (which are normally developed internally by the company) the demand, supply and production plan, which is then dollarized. These plans are not simply the automated first planning output, but are the final plans that have been modified by demand, supply and production planners. Without very much in the way of discussion, some of the newer S&OP applications have broadened out their functionality to the point where they are able to create simplified plans that are already created in supply chain planning systems. However most companies still use spreadsheets for their S&OP process. The more complex and detailed the S&OP application, more categories of data that are sent to it from other systems and the more the S&OP application is able to do on its own. One of the major differentiators between the more traditional S&OP and the more modern S&OP is that the newer applications can capacity level specific resources within the S&OP application, rather than relying upon another system to do this and then send the output to the S&OP application.

The standard S&OP process is to review and sign off on the demand plan, review and sign off on the supply plan and review and sign off on the financial plan. The process begins by trying to develop a final forecast that is the combination of multiple forecasts, as there are multiple forecasts within any company.

When the S&OP system receives the supply plan, it may have been either constrained or capacity leveled. Resource management and constraining is one of the more complex areas of planning, however the objective is to develop a feasible plan. Over the short and perhaps medium-term the company must deal with the constraints that exist. That is the intent of supply chain planning. A big part of short and medium-term supply chain planning is simply moving production and procurement either forward or backwards along the planning timeline in order to eliminate situations of overcapacity. However, S&OP is planning over the long-term and, over the long-term, a company may choose to alter the constraints. While production resources are sometimes constrained or capacity-leveled by supply chain planning systems, the other supply planning focused resources (storage, location, shipping, transportation, etc.) tend not to be. This means that gaining a picture of the overload on these types of resources is much less straightforward. Most companies deal with these types of resources by feel (making educated guesses, based on the intuition of company planners).

This is one of the **myths** of S&OP processes, that all resources are modeled and become part of the S&OP process, allowing for evaluation. However, this is not the case. Even the most advanced supply chain planning applications tend not to focus on supply planning resources (aka, non-production) in isolation. Several software vendors show product demos featuring the management of these types of resources; however, given that this is uncommon even in applications with greater capabilities in the field of resource management, we doubt whether this is a realistic goal.

Finally, while the primary focus tends to be on resources, resources are only one of the constraints in planning, with another example being lot sizes or batch sizes. The final step of the S&OP process is reviewing and finalizing the financial plan. Financial plans are dependent upon the supply plan. For manufacturing and distribution companies, the first obvious financial implication is inventory. For a service company the obvious financial implication is the number of people required for a specific capacity. In addition to how much to increase capacity, a very important question that should come from the S&OP process is when to increase capacity. Almost all capacity is added in discrete rather than continuous units, however, demand tends to change in a continuous fashion, and secondly there is often a lag between the purchase of the capacity and when the capacity is available. The company wants to only add capacity that will have a high utilization, and this may mean doing everything from using outside sources of production, warehousing, etc. before deciding to actually purchase long-term capacity.

Conclusion

This book has focused on both shorter-term and long-term capacity management. Short-to-mid-term capacity planning is performed with capacity leveling and capacity constraining, while longer-term capacity management is performed by capacity planning.

Capacity management is a technical exercise and is one of the most important planning activities that a company does.

1. Various software enables the two categories of capacity management.

2. They are separate processes both because they have different time horizons and because one cannot simultaneously respect the limitations or constraints of a system and question them.

3. With computers, both processes are supported through entering constraints into software and loading the demand -- real or predicted -- upon the constraints.

4. The option in the near- and even mid-term is usually to either "move" the demand by postponing or delaying production from

the time it would ordinarily be scheduled if capacity were unlimited.

5. Controls address a chosen policy to automatically move demand across the planning horizon, such forecast consumption and scheduling direction. These types of control settings are available within **all of the systems** that perform capacity leveling and capacity constraining.

6. The chosen policy for automatically moving demand across alternate resources (which can, in at least one application, be across factories) is addressed by the resource settings within the application. This area is significantly complex.

Generally speaking, capacity leveling is most often performed in with applications that perform MRP as the network or initial planning run. Capacity leveling is then run as part of a procedure or by manual adjustment. Done this way, capacity leveling can be very time consuming and often means that capacity is only leveled at the finished goods level. Therefore, if components or subcomponents are also manufactured internally, the capacity level results in components or subcomponents that **are not leveled**. APS systems do things differently and are better than MRP, and one of the major improvements in APS systems was the ability to **capacity constrain resources**.

In either capacity leveling or capacity constraining, using constraints means setting up inequalities in the system that reduce the solution space to what is feasible. One way of doing this is by adding a resource with capacity. Another way is to add lot sizes, which restrict planned procurement or production to discrete units. The goal is to match constraints as closely as possible to the realities of the environment being modeled.

Different domains of the supply chain have different types of resources that must be modeled. However, while software vendors often discuss the many different categories of resources they can constrain, in the vast majority of cases the only resource category that is constrained are the production resources. This is of course a major issue for creating a truly capacity aware plan because many resources, including labor, **are left out of the calculation**. Often, these resources, including material handling resources, storage resources, etc., are approximated from the volume change, and this is usually performed in spreadsheets. Constraint-based planning works better for manufacturing than for supply planning resources, and it also works better for **some manufacturing environments than others**. Very rarely is this fact regarding the match between application and environment brought up on projects, and it is even more rare for it to be discussed during sales cycles.[1]

With constraint-based planning, three things happen:

1. Resources are declared;

2. At least one of the resources in each process chain has its capacity constrained or capped; and

3. The system can only load the resource up to that cap before moving further loads to a different time or to an alternative resource.

A very important yet under-reported issue of capacity management is how the two major categories of capacity management are **integrated to one another.** And the reason for the under-reporting is that the two types of capacity management tend to be covered as separate subjects. Traditionally, the S&OP system is fed by the output of supply chain planning systems combined with financial data, which includes the price and cost of the item. Having financial information in the system is what allows for budgeting to be (partially) performed. However, while this tells the company its potential gross profit and estimated inventory costs, **a host of other financial considerations are not included in the model**. For example, the costs of new equipment may have to be added and other factors exist as well. Therefore, the best way of looking at S&OP systems is that they provide a portion of the financial data required for budgeting. However, what every organization must determine is how capacity leveling and constraining systems integrate with capacity planning systems. In some cases, the beginning of the **capacity planning process** can be performed in the **capacity leveling and constraining system**. But in most cases, these are two separate systems, and how changes made in an S&OP system migrate back to the lower level planning systems is very important and

---

[1] This is covered in detail in the SCM Focus Press book *Process Industry Manufacturing Software.*

requires careful consideration and design.

One of the most important functions that any organization performs is capacity management. The issue requires dealing with variability and probabilities related to demand and supply combined with financial risk in determining investments. There are many complexities to performing these two categories of capacity management. The first step, however, in understanding capacity management is understanding the difference between its primary processes as well as how they integrate.

References

Integrated Business Planning
Wikipedia, October 15 2015
https://en.wikipedia.org/wiki/Integrated_business_planning

Byrnes, Jonathan. Islands of Profit in a Sea of Red Ink. Portfolio Hardcover. 2010.

http://www.nytimes.com/2013/01/23/us/unfinished-tower-in-las-vegas-is-symbol-of-a-reversal.html

http://www.reviewjournal.com/columns-blogs/inside-gaming/macau-free-fall-and-taking-wynn-resorts-it

http://thetaylorreachgroup.com/2012/04/26/why-most-call-center-customer-service-is-so-bad/

http://www.helpscout.net/75-customer-service-facts-quotes-statistics/

http://www.teslamotors.com/gigafactory

http://www.forbes.com/sites/stevebanker/2015/07/16/sales-operations-planning-continues-to-evolve/

Olhager, Jan. Rudgerg, Martin. Wikner, Joakim. Long Term Capacity Management: Linking the Perspectives from Manufacturing Strategy and Sales Operations Planning. International Journal of Production Economics. 2001.

Hagemeyer,Dale. *Vendor Panorama for Trade Promotion Management in Consumer Goods.* Gartner, 2012.

Lucas, Anthony. "In-Store Trade Promotions – Profit or Loss?" *Journal of Consumer Marketing.* April 1, 1996.

http://www.boozallen.com/media/file/Lessons_From_The_Shop_Floor.pdf

Wacker, G John.Lummus, Ronda R. Sales Forecasting for Strategic Resource Planning. International Journal of Operations and Production Management. 2002.

http://theplanningblog.com/integrating-the-sop-process-go-with-the-flow/

http://clarkstonconsulting.com/wp-content/uploads/2015/04/IBP_SupplyChain.pdf

https://www.youtube.com/watch?v=h4tbejP4rkE

Stahley, Tim. From Misery to Mastery: *How to Build a Better Sales Forecast.* http://www.right90.com/whitepapers/Misery_to_Mastery_White%20Paper_10_14NO-CHANGES.pdf.

Right90. *7 Secrets of Sales Forecasting.* http://www.right90.com/whitepapers/7_secrets_of_sales_forecastingFINALPRINT.pdf.

Guido Grüne, Stephanie Lockemann, Volker Kluy. Business Process Management within Chemical and Pharmaceutical Industries. Springer Press. 2013

Snapp, Shaun. Forecast Parameters: Alpha, Beta Gamma, etc..SCM Focus Press. 2014.

Snapp, Shaun. Superplant: Creating a Nimble Manufacturing Enterprise with Adaptive Planning Software.SCM Focus Press. 2013.

Snapp, Shaun. Inventory Optimization and Multi Echelon Software.SCM Focus Press. 2012.

Snapp, Shaun. Constrained Supply and Production Planning in SAP APO. SCM Focus Press. 2013.

Snapp, Shaun. Replenishment Triggers: Setting Systems for Make to Stock, Make to Order & Assemble to Order. SCM Focus Press. 2015.

Snapp, Shaun. Sales and Operations Planning in Software. SCM Focus Press. 2016.

http://www.mobiusuk.co.uk/articles/2012/11/16/sales-and-operations-planning-how-to-avoid-the-5-key-pitfalls/

https://www.sapstore.com/solutions/60032/SAP-Integrated-Business-Planning-for-sales-and-operations

Sales and Operations Planning, October 9 2015
https://en.wikipedia.org/wiki/Sales_and_operations_planning

Capacity Planning, November 12 2015
https://en.wikipedia.org/wiki/Capacity_planning

Author Profile

Shaun Snapp is the founder and editor of SCM Focus. SCM Focus is one of the largest independent supply chain software analysis and educational sites on the Internet.

After working at several of the largest consulting companies and at i2 Technologies, he became an independent consultant and later started SCM Focus. He maintains a strong interest in comparative software design, and works both in SAP APO as well as with a variety of best-of-breed supply chain planning vendors. His ongoing relationships with these vendors keep him on the cutting edge of emerging technology.

Primary Sources of Information and Writing Topics

Shaun writes about topics with which he has firsthand experience. These topics range from recovering problematic implementations, to system configuration, to socializing complex software and supply chain concepts in the areas of demand planning, supply planning and production planning.

More broadly, he writes on topics supportive of these applications, which include master data parameter management, integration, analytics, simulation and bill of material management systems. He covers management aspects of enterprise software ranging from software policy to handling consulting partners on SAP projects.

Shaun writes from an implementer's perspective and as a result he focuses on how software is actually used in practice rather than its hypothetical or "pure release note capabilities." Unlike many authors in enterprise software who keep their distance from discussing the realities of software implementation, he writes both on the problems as well as the successes of his software use. This gives him a distinctive voice in the field.

Secondary Sources of Information

In addition to project experience, Shaun's interest in academic literature is a secondary source of information for his books and articles. Intrigued with the historical perspective of supply chain software, much of his writing is influenced by his readings and research into how different categories of supply chain software developed, evolved, and finally became broadly used over time.

Covering the Latest Software Developments

Shaun is focused on supply chain software selections and implementation improvement through writing and consulting, bringing companies some of the newest technologies and methods. Some of the software developments that Shaun showcases at SCM Focus and in books at SCM Focus Press have yet to reach widespread adoption.

Education

Shaun has an undergraduate degree in business from the University of Hawaii, a Master of Science in Maritime Management from the Maine Maritime Academy and a Master of Science in Business Logistics from Penn State University. He has taught both logistics and SAP software.

Software Certifications

Shaun has been trained and/or certified in products from i2 Technologies, Servigistics, ToolsGroup and SAP (SD, DP, SNP, SPP, EWM).

Contact

Shaun can be contacted at: shaunsnapp@scmfocus.com

Abbreviations

DRP – Distribution Requirements Planning
ERP – Enterprise Resource Planning
MEIO – Inventory Optimization and Multi Echelon Planning Software
MRP – Material Requirements Planning
S&OP – Sales and Operations Planning

Links Listed in the Book by Chapter

Chapter 1:

http://www.scmfocus.com/writing-rules/

http://www.scmfocus.com/

Chapter 2:

http://www.scmfocus.com/sapplanning/2009/07/01/bottleneck-resources/

http://www.scmfocus.com/supplyplanning/2011/10/02/commonly-used-and-unused-constraints-for-supply-planning/

http://www.scmfocus.com/sapplanning/2008/05/08/capacity-leveling-in-snp/

http://www.scmfocus.com/sapplanning/2008/05/08/capacity-planning-and-constraint-based-planning-for-service-parts/

Chapter 3

http://www.scmfocus.com/sapplanning/2009/07/01/bottleneck-resources/

http://www.scmfocus.com/supplyplanning/2011/10/02/commonly-used-and-unused-constraints-for-supply-planning/

http://www.scmfocus.com/supplychainmasterdata/2011/05/methodology-for-adjusting-master-data/

Chapter 4

http://www.scmfocus.com/sapplanning/2009/05/02/scm-resource-types/

http://www.scmfocus.com/sapplanning/2012/12/06/the-goods-receipt-processing-time-and-the-handling-resource/

http://www.scmfocus.com/sapplanning/2012/08/19/time-continuous-planning-versus-bucket-in-ctm-and-ppds/

http://www.scmfocus.com/supplychaininnovation/2009/06/google-maps-and-gomobileiq-for-vehicle-routing/

http://www.scmfocus.com/fourthpartylogistics/2012/04/the-overestimation-of-outsourced-logistics/

http://www.scmfocus.com/productionplanningandscheduling/2012/08/25/the-over-generalization-of-discrete-manufacturing-inventory-management/

http://www.scmfocus.com/sapplanning/2011/11/05/how-soft-constraints-work-with-soft-constraints-days-supply-and-safety-stock-penalty-costs/

Chapter 5

http://www.scmfocus.com/sapplanning/2012/06/27/backward-scheduling-forward-scheduling-sap-erp-sap-apo/

http://www.scmfocus.com/sapplanning/2012/06/13/front-loading-resources-in-sap-snp/

http://www.scmfocus.com/sapplanning/2012/08/08/effective-resource-front-loading-with-maximum-earliness-or-sequential-ctm-profiles/

http://www.scmfocus.com/sapplanning/2008/09/21/ppds-and-snp-heuristics/